COLLEGE ALGEBRA

CLEP* Study Guide

© 2019 Breely Crush Publishing, LLC

*CLEP is a registered trademark of the College Entrance Examination Board which does not endorse this book.

971091518143

Published by Breely Crush Publishing, LLC
10808 River Front Parkway
South Jordan, UT 84095
www.breelycrushpublishing.com

ISBN-10: 1-61433-562-1
ISBN-13: 978-1-61433-562-7

Printed and bound in the United States of America.

Table of Contents

Algebraic Operations

What is an algebraic expression? Expressions contain numbers and variables that are called "terms." An algebraic expression does **NOT** have an equal sign. It is simply a collection of terms that are separated by arithmetic operations including addition, subtraction, multiplication, and division.

How do you combine algebraic expressions? There are three main steps involved in combining (or simplifying) an algebraic expression. The three steps include:

1. Identify "like" terms.
2. Add or subtract the coefficients of "like" terms.
3. Multiply the number found in Step 2 by the common variable(s).

In order to complete these three steps, you need to understand a few definitions:

"Like" terms: Two terms are considered "like" terms if they have the **SAME** variable with the **SAME** exponent. For example, 2x and 3x are like terms because they have the same variable "x" and this variable has the same exponent of 1.

Following is a table that contains "like" terms and "unlike" terms:

"LIKE" TERMS	"UNLIKE" TERMS
$2y, -14y$	$2y, -14x$
$3x^2, 12x^2$	$3x^2, 3x$
$14, -14$	$14, -14z$
$\frac{1}{2}x^4, 2x^4$	$\frac{1}{2}y^4, 2x^4$
$0.75x, 15x$	$0.75x, 15xy^2$

Coefficient of the Variable: The coefficient of the variable is the number that is multiplied by the variable. In other words, the coefficient of the variable is the number directly in front of the variable. For example, the coefficient of 3x is 3 and the coefficient of 0.75y is 0.75.

The coefficient of the variable is sometimes referred to as the "Numerical Coefficient" and it can be positive, negative, an Integer, fraction, or decimal.

Examples of Combining Algebraic Expressions:

1. $2x + 3x$ Answer: $5x$

2. $10y + 9 + 14y - 5$ Answer: $24y + 4$

3. $3x^2 + 2x - 5x^2 + 6y$ Answer: $-2x^2 + 2x + 6y$

What are Polynomials? A polynomial is an expression containing the sum of a finite number of terms of the form **ax^n**, for any real number **a** and any whole number **n**.

Examples of Polynomials:

$$x^2 + 6x + 5$$

$$2x^3 + 3x^2 + 4x + 16$$

How do you ADD and SUBTRACT two polynomials?
There are two general steps you take to add and subtract polynomials. The two steps include:

       Step #1: Remove parentheses

       Step #2: Combine "like" terms

Question: Evaluate $(x^2 + 8x + 12) + (2x^2 - 3x + 13)$
This is an ADDITION problem.

       1. Remove the parentheses
Note: There is a positive 1 on the outside of each parenthesis.
Therefore, you multiply a positive 1 by each term to remove the parentheses.

$$1(x^2 + 8x + 12) + 1(2x^2 - 3x + 13)$$
$$x^2 + 8x + 12 + 2x^2 - 3x + 13$$

2. Combine "like" terms

$$x^2 + 2x^2 + 8x - 3x + 12 + 13$$

Answer: $3x^2 + 5x + 25$

Question: Evaluate $(x^2 + 8x + 12) - (2x^2 - 3x + 13)$
This is a SUBTRACTION problem.

1. Remove the parentheses

Note: There is a positive one by the first set of parentheses, but a NEGATIVE one by the second set of parentheses because you are dealing with subtraction. The signs of the first polynomial remain the same and change the signs of the second polynomial to their opposites.

$$(x^2 + 8x + 12) - (2x^2 - 3x + 13)$$
$$1(x^2 + 8x + 12) - 1(2x^2 - 3x + 13)$$
$$x^2 + 8x + 12 - 2x^2 + 3x + 13$$

2. Combine "like" terms

$$x^2 - 2x^2 + 8x + 3x + 12 - 13$$
Answer: $-x^2 + 11x - 1$

How do I multiply two terms that have variables with exponents?

You will need to know the "Rules of Exponents" to multiply two terms that have variables with exponents. To use these rules you **MUST** have the **SAME** Variable.

Basic rules of exponents:

Product Rule: When multiplying two terms, just **ADD** their exponents and **MULTIPLY** their coefficients.

Question:

$$2x^3 \times 3x^4$$
$$(2 \times 3)(x^3 \times x^4)$$
Answer: $6x^7$

Quotient Rule: When dividing two terms, just **SUBTRACT** their exponents and **DIVIDE** their coefficients. Note: You MUST subtract the bottom exponent from the top exponent.

Question: $\dfrac{2x^{10}}{x^2}$

Answer: $2x^8$

Power Rule: Use this rule when a term is inside parentheses AND raised to a power. In this case you would **MULTIPLY** the exponents and coefficients by the power on the outside of the parentheses.

Question:

$(2x^5)^3$

$(2)^3(x^5)^3$

Answer: $8x^{15}$

How do you MULTIPLY AND DIVIDE two polynomials?

Two types of multiplication include:

- Multiplication using the Distributive property.
- Multiplication of two binomials using the FOIL method.

How to multiply terms using the Distributive Property:

Evaluate: $2x(x + 14)$

Multiply the term "$2x$" by **EACH** term on the inside of the parentheses.

Question:

$2x(x + 14)$

$2x(x) + 2x(14)$

Answer: $2x^2 + 28x$

How do you multiply two binomials using the "FOIL" method?

Use the FOIL method to multiply two binomials.

Question: Evaluate $(x + 3)(x + 4)$
Multiply **F**irst Terms: $(\boldsymbol{x} + 3)(\boldsymbol{x} + 4) = x^2$
Multiply **O**uter Terms: $(\boldsymbol{x} + 3)(x + \boldsymbol{4}) = 4x$
Multiply **I**nner Terms: $(x + \boldsymbol{3})(\boldsymbol{x} + 4) = 3x$
Multiply **L**ast Terms: $(x + \boldsymbol{3})(x + \boldsymbol{4}) = 12$

Therefore, $x^2 + 4x + 3x + 12$
Combine "like" terms:
Answer: $x^2 + 7x + 12$

What does it mean to "FACTOR" a polynomial? Remember how to factor a number? Factors are two numbers or terms that when multiplied together yield the original term. You will be given a Polynomial in Standard Form such as $x^2 + 7x + 12$. Factoring this polynomial is the reverse of applying the distributive property.

For example, Factors of the number 12 include:
1 x 12
2 x 6
3 x 4

The same method applies to Polynomials; however you have to take into account the Rules of Exponents.

For example, the factors of $2x^2$ can be 2 and x^2 because when you multiply the two factors together you end up with your original $2x^2$.

How do you factor a polynomial (trinomial) of the form $x^2 + bx + c$?
Follow these two steps:

1. Find all possible pairs of integers whose product is **c**.
2. For each pair, test whether its sum is **b**.

Question: Factor $x^2 + 7x + 12$
What factors of "12" add up to "7"? The factors 3 and 4 fit the criteria.
Answer: $(x + 3)(x + 4)$

How do you factor a polynomial (trinomial) of the form $ax^2 + bx + c$?

Follow these three steps:

1. Compute **ac** for all the possible factors of **a** and **c**. Find all the possible pairs of integers (positive and negative) whose product is **ac**.
2. For each pair of integers, test if its sum is **b**.
3. If the pair of integers satisfies both step 1 and step 2 then you will use those factors.

Question: Factor $2x^2 + 11x + 5$

ac = 10. The factors of 5 are 1 and 5. Therefore, you must put the factors in the correct order. You can double check your answer by using the foil method.

Answer: $(2x + 1)(x + 5)$

How do you simplify algebraic fractions? An algebraic fraction occurs when you have one algebraic expression above another algebraic expression. In other words, the algebraic expressions are expressed as a quotient.

For example, $\dfrac{2x^2 + 12x}{2x}$ and $\dfrac{x^2 + 4x + 3}{x + 1}$.

If the algebraic fraction has a one term (a monomial) in the denominator then you simply divide EACH term in the numerator expression by the denominator. Note: Use the Quotient rule for the exponents.

Question:

$$\frac{2x^2 + 12x}{2x} \rightarrow \frac{2x^2}{2x} + \frac{12x}{2x}$$

Answer: $x + 6$

If the algebraic fraction has two terms (a binomial) in the denominator then you will need to simplify using long division.

Question:

$$\frac{x^2 + 4x + 3}{x + 1}$$

$x^2 + 4x + 3$ is the "dividend". $x + 1$ is the "divisor".

Write the fraction as a division problem in the following form:

$$x + 2 \overline{)x^2 + 6x + 8}$$

Divide x^2 (the first term in the dividend) by x (the first term in the divisor).

$$\frac{x^2}{x} = x \quad \rightarrow \quad x + 2 \overline{)x^2 + 6x + 8} \;\overset{x}{}$$

Multiply x by $x + 2$ and subtract this from the dividend. Bring down the next term.

$$\begin{array}{r} x \\ x + 2 \overline{)x^2 + 6x + 8} \\ \underline{-x^2 - 2x} \\ 4x + 8 \end{array}$$

Repeat the process.

$$\begin{array}{r} x + 4 \\ x + 2 \overline{)x^2 + 6x + 8} \\ \underline{-x^2 - 2x} \\ 4x + 8 \\ \underline{-4x - 8} \\ 0 \end{array}$$

Answer: $x + 4$

☞ Equations, Inequalities and Their Graphs

What is an algebraic equation? Equations contain numbers and variables that are called "terms". An algebraic equation must have an equal sign. Equations must always be in "balance" meaning that the value of each side of the equation is the same.

How do you solve a Linear equation? You need to follow specific procedures when solving an equation. The two main goals you need to accomplish include moving the variable to one side of the equal sign and setting the coefficient of the variable equal to 1.

Example of a "One" Step Linear Equation: Solve $x + 10 = 28$

The variable "x" already has a coefficient of 1 so we need to move 10 to the other side of the equation. Therefore, you will add the opposite of 10 to each side of the equation. Remember: When you complete an operation on one side of the equation you MUST do the exact same operation to the other side of the equation.

$x + 10 = 28$

$x + (10 - 10) = (28 - 10)$

$x + 0 = 18$

$x = 18$

Example of a "Two" Step Linear Equation: Solve $2x + 15 = 45$

First, move 15 to the other side of the equation so that $2x$ is by itself on one side.

$2x + 15 = 45$

$2x + (15 - 15) = (45 - 15)$

$2x = 30$

The second step is to make the coefficient of the variable 1. Therefore, divide each side by 2.

$2x = 30$

$$\frac{2x}{2} = \frac{30x}{2} = 15$$

Therefore, $x = 15$

Note: Dividing by 2 is the equivalent to multiplying its reciprocal of ½.

Example of "Two" Step Linear Equation using a Reciprocal: Solve $\frac{2}{3}x + 2 = 8$

$$\frac{2}{3}x + 2 = 8$$

$$\frac{2}{3}x + (2 - 2) = (8 - 2)$$

$$\frac{2}{3}x = 6$$

$$\frac{3}{2} * \frac{2}{3}x = 6 * \frac{3}{2}$$

$$x = 9$$

How do you graph Linear Equations in TWO variables?
You can think of each "x" and "y" value as an **ordered pair (x,y)** in a graph.

Follow these five steps:
1. Solve the equation for y. (This means to have y by itself on one side and have a coefficient of 1.)
2. Arbitrarily pick a value for x.
3. Plug that x value into the equation and solve for y.
4. Repeat this process until you have a minimum of three ordered pairs.
5. Draw a straight line to connect the plotted points.

Question*:* Graph $x + y = 10$

1.) Solve the equation for y by moving "x" to the other side of the equation. Since the x term is positive then we subtract x from each side.

$$x + y = 10$$
$$(x - x) + y = (10 - x)$$
$$y = 10 - x$$

2.) Arbitrarily pick a value for x.

3.) Plug it into the equation to find y.

Let's try $x = 0$.

$$y = 10 - x$$
$$y = 10 - 0$$
$$y = 10$$

Therefore, our first ordered pair is (0, 10).

4.) Repeat the process until you have a minimum of three ordered pairs.

Try $x = 1$

$$y = 10 - x$$
$$y = 10 - 1$$
$$y = 9$$

Therefore, our second ordered pair is $(1, 9)$.

Try $x = 2$

$$y = 10 - x$$
$$y = 10 - 2$$
$$y = 8$$

Therefore, our third ordered pair is $(2, 8)$.

5.) Draw a straight line to connect the plotted points. Here is the graph you should have created.

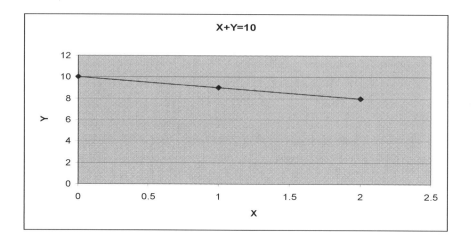

Quadratic Equations

What is a quadratic equation? A quadratic equation in one variable is an equation that can be changed into the form $ax^2 + bx + c = 0$, where a, b, and c are real constants. A **solution** to a quadratic equation is always a **root** of the polynomial $ax^2 + bx + c = 0$.

How do you find the "root" of a polynomial? The roots of a polynomial can be found by **factoring** the polynomial. Set each factor equal to "0" and solve the equation.

> **Question:** Find the solutions to the Quadratic equation: $x^2 + 7x + 12$
>
> Factor to find: $(x + 3)(x + 4)$
>
> $x + 3 = 0$ Therefore $x = -3$
>
> $x + 4 = 0$ Therefore $x = -4$
>
> The solutions are -3 and -4.

How do you solve a quadratic equation using the "square root" property? The square root property says that if you set $x^2 = a$ then $x = \pm\sqrt{a}$.

> **Question:** Solve $x^2 = 36$
> **Answer:** $x = \pm\sqrt{36} = \pm6$

How do you solve a quadratic equation by completing the square? When you solve a quadratic equation by completing the square you are creating a trinomial that can be expressed as a square of a binomial.

Follow these seven steps to solve a quadratic equation by completing the square.

1. Use the multiplication (or division) property of equality if necessary to make the numerical coefficient of the squared term equal to 1.

2. Rewrite the equation with the constant by itself on the right side of the equation.

3. Take one-half the numerical coefficient of the first-degree term, square it, and add this quantity to both sides of the equation.

4. Replace the trinomial with its equivalent squared binomial.

5. Use the square root property.

6. Solve for the variable.

7. Check your answers with the original equation.

Question: Solve $x^2 - 10x + 21$ by completing the square.

1. $x^2 - 10x + 21 = 0$

2. $x^2 - 10x = -21$

3. $\frac{1}{2}(-10) = -5$ and $(-5)^2 = 25$

   $x^2 - 10x + 25 = -21 + 25$

   $x^2 - 10x + 25 = 4$

4. $(x - 5)^2 = 4$

5. $x - 5 = \pm\sqrt{4}$ Therefore, $x - 5 = \pm 2$

How do you solve a quadratic equation by using the quadratic formula?
Follow these two steps:

1. Write the equation in standard form, $ax^2 + bx + c = 0$, and determine the numerical values for a, b, and c.

2. Substitute the values for a, b, and c from Step 1 in the quadratic formula below and then evaluate to obtain the solution.

THE QUADRATIC FORMULA:

$$x = \frac{-b \pm \sqrt{b^2 - 4ac}}{2a}$$

How do you graph a quadratic equation? The graph of a quadratic equation is a parabola. You can graph a quadratic equation by setting $y = ax^2 + bx + c$. Arbitrarily pick a value for x, plug this into the equation to find y. Graph the coordinate pairs.

Note: If "a" is positive then the parabola will open upward. If "a" is negative then the parabola will open downward. The "vertex" of the parabola is the lowest point on the parabola that opens upward or the highest point on the parabola that opens downward. A parabola should be symmetric with a vertical line of symmetry that splits the two halves of the parabola.

Note: You can find the vertex of the parabola using $x = -\dfrac{b}{2a}$ and $y = \dfrac{4ac - b^2}{4a}$

Question: Graph $y = x^2$

If $x = 3$ then $y = 9$. If $x = 4$ then $y = 16$. If $x = 5$ then $y = 25$.
If $x = -3$ then $y = 9$. If $x = -4$ then $y = 16$. If $x = -5$ then $y = 25$.

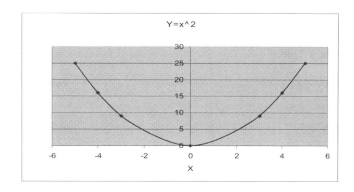

What are systems of Linear Equations? Systems of equations contain more then one equation. Solutions to a system of equations satisfy ALL the equations.

How do you find solutions to a system of Linear Equations?
Solve systems of linear equations by using the "Addition Method".
Follow these six steps:

1. If necessary, rewrite each equation so that the terms containing variables appear on the left hand side of the equal sign and any constants appear on the right side of the equal sign.

2. If necessary, multiply one or both equations by a constant(s) so that when the equations are added the resulting sum will contain only one variable.

3. Add the equations. This will yield a single equation containing only one variable.

4. Solve for the variable in the equation from step 3.

5. a) Substitute the value found in step 4 into either of the original equations. Solve that equation to find the value of the remaining variable.
OR
   b) Repeat steps 2-4 to eliminate the other variable.

6. Check the values obtained in all original equations.

Question: Solve $x + 3y = 13$ (Equation 1)

$\qquad\qquad x + 4y = 18$ (Equation 2)

Multiply Equation 1 by -1.

$-1(x + 3y) = -1(13) \quad \rightarrow \quad -x - 3y = -13$

Add Equation 1 and Equation 2

$-x - 3y = -13$

$\underline{x + 4y = 18}$

$\qquad\quad y = 5$

Note: In this case both x variables had a coefficient of 1, allowing them to be combined to equal zero. In some cases it may be necessary to multiply the equation by a constant in order to achieve this.

Plug $y = 5$ into the original equation 1 to find $x = -2$. Check that this solution satisfies both equations.

How do you graph systems of linear equations? Simply graph a line for each linear equation.

What is absolute value? Absolute value refers to the distance between a number and 0 on the number line. Absolute value is always positive.

What is the notation for Absolute Value and how do we find it?

The notation for absolute value is $|\ |$.

You change the sign of the number inside the $|\ |$ to a positive number.

Examples of Absolute Value:

$$|-2| = 2 \qquad |4| = 4 \qquad \left|\frac{-3}{4}\right| = \frac{3}{4}$$

Note: $-|-2| = -2$

Question: Find the solutions for $|3x - 5| = 2x$.

If $2x \geq 0$ then $3x - 5 = 2x$ where $x = 5$

OR $3x - 5 = -2x$ where $x = 1$.

How do you graph a circle? The equation for a circle with a center point at (0,0) follows the general form of $x^2 + y^2 = r^2$ where "r" is the radius of the circle. If the center point of the circle is NOT at (0,0) then use the equation $(x - h)^2 + (y - k)^2 = r^2$ where "h" is the horizontal distance x from the origin and "k" is the vertical distance y from the origin. The center of the circle, therefore, will be (h,k).

> **Question:** What is the center and radius of the circle $(x + 2)^2 + (y - 4)^2 = 81$? Center C(–2,4), and radius r = 9.

 # Simple Transformations of Functions

What is Symmetry? Many graphs can be described as symmetric. A graph can be symmetric about the y-axis, the x-axis, and the origin. A graph which is symmetric about the y-axis will have the same y coordinate when evaluating $f(x)$ as when evaluating $f(-x)$ (See example a). A graph which is symmetric about the x-axis would have points appearing at both (x, y) and (x, –y) (see example b). Therefore the graph which is symmetric about the x-axis is not a function. A graph which is symmetric about the origin will have opposite values of y coordinates when evaluating $f(x)$ and $f(-x)$ (see example c).

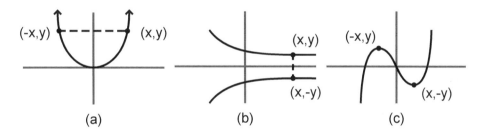

(a)   (b)   (c)

What are Translations? A translation is when the shape of the function is kept the same, but it is shifted to a different place on the coordinate graph.

A vertical translation is when the graph shifts up or down on the y-axis. Vertical translations occur when a number is added to the end of the function.

For example:

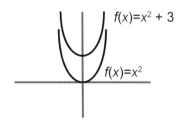

$f(x)=x^2 + 3$

$f(x)=x^2$

A horizontal translation is when the graph shifts right or left along the x-axis. Horizontal transformations occur when a number is added after the x, but still inside the square.

For example, the graphs of $y = x^2$ and $y = (x+3)^2$

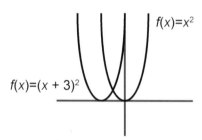

What are Reflections? A reflection is when the graph of a function is mirrored onto another part of the graph. Generally reflections occur across either the x-or y-axis. A graph will be symmetric across the line it is reflected over.

The graph of $y = -f(x)$ is the same as the graph of $y = f(x)$ reflected across the x-axis. For example, $y = x^2$ and $y = -x^2$

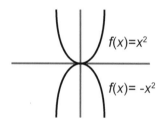

 # Algebraic Inequalities

What are the four equality signs? Read the following signs from left to right.
< is "less than"
> is "greater than"
≤ is "less than or equal to"
≥ is "greater than or equal to"

You can use inequality signs in an algebraic equation format.

How do you solve and graph Linear Inequalities in ONE variable?
Solve and graph $x < 4$ on a number line.

In equalities you will have more than one possible value for the variable x. This inequality is "solved" because x is on one side by itself and has a coefficient of 1. Therefore, you can go right to graphing it on a number line.

In this example, every number less than and NOT including 4 is a possible value. Since 4 is NOT a possible value for *x* then you will leave an OPEN circle at 4. Shade in the values less than 4 to represent all the possible values for *x*. Remember to shade in the arrow as well indicating that the possible values go on into negative infinity.

$$x < 4$$

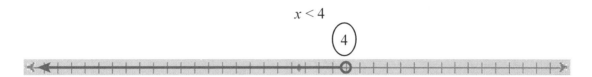

Linear Inequality Example: Solve and graph $x + 10 < 5$
Solve this as you would an equation keeping the < sign in tact.

$$x + 10 < 5$$
$$x + (10 - 10) < (5 - 10)$$
$$x < -5$$

Linear Inequality Example: Solve and graph $2x + 4 \geq 10$

$$2x + 4 \quad 10$$
$$2x + (4 - 4) \geq (10 - 4)$$
$$2x \geq 6$$
$$\frac{2x}{2} \geq \frac{6}{2}$$
$$x \geq 3$$

Note: Since the inequality sign is "greater than or equal to" we MUST include 3 on our number line. Therefore, you need to shade in the circle at $x = 3$.

Special Rule when solving Inequalities: There is one special rule that you need to use when you have a "–x" value to begin with. Remember that we want x to be positive and have a coefficient of 1. In the very last step of the inequality you divide each side of the inequality by a negative number. This means that you need to change the direction of the inequality sign to the opposite direction. This is ONLY when dividing (or multiplying by a reciprocal) by a NEGATIVE number.

Special Rule Linear Inequality Example: Solve and graph $-2x < 10$.

$$-2x < 10$$

$$\frac{-2x}{-2} < \frac{10}{-2}$$

$$x > -5$$

How do you graph linear inequalities in TWO variables? Graph the linear inequality. Choose a test point above (or below) the line. The test point must NOT be on the line. If the test point is below the line and the test point satisfies the equation then you shade the region below the graphed line. If the test point below the graphed line does NOT satisfy the graphed line then you shade the region above the graphed line.

Note: If the inequality is < or > then the graphed line is DOTTED.
If the inequality is ≤ or ≥ then the graphed line is SOLID.

Question: Graph $3x + 4y < 12$

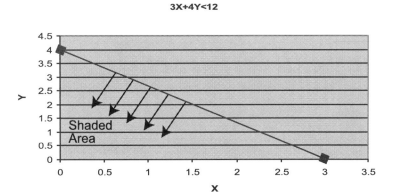

3X+4Y<12

Test Point (0,0). Does (0,0) satisfy $3x + 4y < 12$?
Yes because $0 < 12$. Therefore, shade BELOW the graphed line.

How do you graph systems of linear inequalities? Graph each linear inequality on the same axes. The solution is the set of points that satisfies all the inequalities in the system. In other words, the solution is the region where the shaded regions from each inequality overlap.

Absolute Value Equations and Inequalities

What is an absolute value? Absolute value refers to the distance between a number and 0 on the number line. Because distance cannot be negative, absolute values are always positive.

What is the notation for absolute value and how do we find it? The notation for absolute value is two vertical lines with the terms you wish to find the absolute value of in between them. For example, $|x - 5|$ indicates that you should find the absolute value of "x–5". An absolute value is found by making sure that whatever is inside the absolute value becomes positive. If it is negative, change it to a positive. If it is positive, leave it as it is.

Examples of finding absolute values:

$|-2| = 2$ $|4| = 4$ $|5 - 10| = 5$ $-|1| = -1$

Absolute values in equations: Absolute values can also be found in equations and graphed. The graph of an absolute value will always appear like a "V". For example, the equation appears as a "V" with the vertex, or point, at the origin (pictured below). You can graph absolute values by plugging in values for x, and finding the corresponding y values, as you would with any other type of graph.

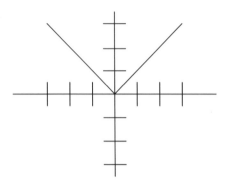

Solving single-variable equations with absolute values: To solve an equation with an absolute value in it use the following two steps:

1. Get the absolute value on one side of the equals sign, with everything else opposite.
2. Solve the inside of the absolute value for both the positive and negative form of whatever is on the other side of the equals sign.

Absolute values will always have two solutions. The positive form of what it is equal to and the negative form. This is because the absolute value will turn any negatives positive.

Example of solving an absolute value equation: Solve

Step #1: Get the absolute value alone:

$$|x + 5| - 4 = -3$$
$$|x + 5| = 1$$

Step #2: Solve for the positive and negative forms of the answer:

$$x + 5 = 1$$
$$x = -4$$

$$x + 5 = -1$$
$$x = -6$$

Therefore, $x = 4, -6$.

Note: This can be verified by plugging the answers back into the original equation.

Inequalities and absolute values: When there is an inequality in an absolute value equation, treat it like you with any other time an inequality is in an equation. They can be graphed on a coordinate grid, in which case you just need to plug in numbers to determine which part of the graph to shade, or they can be plotted on a number line. Note: Because absolute values have more than one possibility, they may have two different shaded areas on a number line.

Example of a single-variable inequality with an absolute value: Solve and graph $|x - 1| > 2$.

Answer: Because the absolute value is already alone, we can move straight to solving for x. However, there is a special trick. Solve for the positive value "2" as normal. However, when solving for the negative value "–2" change the inequality around as shown below:

$x - 1 > 2$
$x > 3$

$x - 1 < -2$
$x < -1$

Therefore, the graph will appear:

Parallel and Perpendicular Lines

What are parallel lines? Two lines are parallel if they lie in the same plane and never intersect. Parallel lines are denoted by the $||$ symbol.

Line 1 ⟷

Line 2 ⟷   Line 1 $||$ **Line 2**

What are perpendicular lines? Two lines are perpendicular if their intersection forms a right angle. Perpendicular lines are denoted by the ⊥.

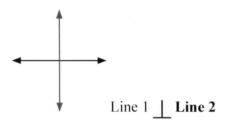

Line 1 ⊥ **Line 2**

🎓 *Functions and Their Graphs*

What is a function? A mathematical function represents a systematic manner in which to find a *value*. In other words, when you input information into a function you will generate a specific "unique" output. A function is usually written as $f(x)$.

For example, let's look at the function: $f(x) = x + 2$ and the value of $x = 3$

The Input is the value $x = 3$ while the output will be what you find when you plug "3" in for x in the equation $f(x) = x + 2$.

$$f(x) = x + 2$$
$$f(3) = 3 + 2$$
$$\text{Therefore, } f(3) = 5$$

Can you figure out what the value of $f(10)$ given $f(x) = x + 2$?

$$f(x) = x + 2$$
$$f(10) = 10 + 2$$
$$\text{Therefore, } f(10) = 12$$

How do functions relate to graphing? Functions pair up x values with y values. Functions must have only one y (or output) value for each x (or input).

What are domain and range? Once it has been determined if a graph can be defined as a function, then domain and range can be used to further define the graph. Domain refers to the set of x values that can be input into an equation, and range refers to the set of y values to which the graph can be equal.

What is the domain of a function? The domain of a function refers to all the possible values you can use for "*x*" in the function $f(x)$ otherwise known as the first number in each ordered pair. The function $f(x) = 2x$ produced the following ordered pairs: (**–1**, –2), (**0**,0), (**1**,2), (**2**,4), (**3**,6). The domain is represented by the bold numbers which are {–1, 0, 1, 2, and 3}.

What is the range of a function? The range of a function refers to all the possible values you can determine for the output $f(x)$ or "*y*". The range from the previous $f(x) = 2x$ is the second number in each ordered pair. (–1,–2), (0,0), (1,2), (2,4), (3,6). Therefore, the range is {–2, 0, 2, 4, 6}.

How are domain and range expressed? Domain and range are generally expressed using brackets and parenthesis. For example if the range for a particular function includes 0 and goes to infinity, it would be expressed as [0,∞). The bracket indicates that the 0 is included in the range. A parentheses indicates that a number is not included in the range, and is always used in the case of infinity because it is cannot be reached. Domain and range can also be expressed as an equation or inequality. For example if the domain of the function includes all real numbers, but excludes the number two, the domain could be written as $x \neq 2$. Generally, however, this sort of notation is avoided and instead the union sign is used. In the case of the domain being all real numbers except 2, it would be expressed $(-\infty, 2) \cup (2, \infty)$.

Example 1: Consider the equation $y = \dfrac{1}{x}$.

The domain of the equation is $(-\infty, 0) \cup (0, \infty)$, because $x \neq 0$. Dividing by 0 is undefined.

The range of this equation is $(-\infty, \infty)$, because the graph continues to both positive and negative infinity in the *y* direction.

Example 2: Consider the equation $y = x^2$.

The domain of the equation is $(-\infty, \infty)$

The range of the equation is [0,∞) because y will always be greater than 0, but goes to infinity as *x* does.

How can you tell if a graph represents a function? Use the "vertical line test" to determine if a graph represents a function. The vertical line test states that if you draw a vertical line through a piece of the graph and it intersects the graph at one more than one point then it is NOT a function. (Remember for every "*x*" value you can have only ONE "*y*" value in order for the relationship to be a function.)

Following is a visual representation to explain the vertical line test.

$f(x) = x^2$ is a function as the red vertical line passes through the graph at only one y value.

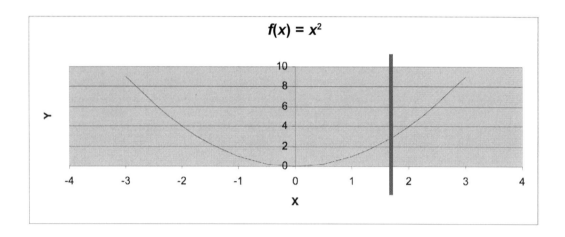

The following graph is NOT a function because the red vertical line passes through more than one *y* value.

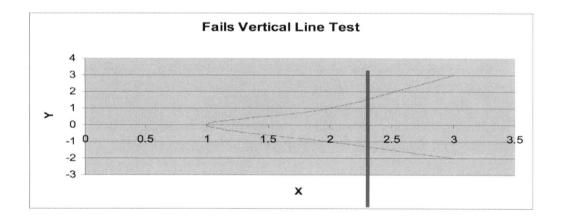

How do you find the Composition of two functions? The composition of two functions takes the terms of one function and substitutes them into the other function. The composition of two functions is denoted as $f(g(x))$.

For example, find $f(g(x))$

When $f(x) = x^2 + 10$ and $g(x) = 3x$

$f(g(x)) = f(3x) = (3x)^2 + 10 = 9x^2 + 10$

Therefore, $f(g(x)) = 9x^2 + 10$

How do you find the Inverse of a function? The inverse of a function can be found by switching the x variable with the y variable. For example, let $y = f(x) = x^2$ then the inverse is denoted as f^{-1} is $f^{-1}(x) = f(y) = y^2$.

 # *Finding the Inverse of Functions*

Inverse functions are pairs of functions that can reverse the effect of each other. To find an inverse function, you must interchange the domain and range. In other words, switch the x and y values.

If the original function is $f(x)$ then the inverse is denoted as $f^{-1}(x)$.

Example 1: Find the inverse of $f(x) = 3x + 5$.

Answer:

Step #1: Set $y = 3x + 5$

Step #2: Interchange x and y to get $x = 3y + 5$

Step #3: Solve for y to get $f^{-1}(x)$.

$x = 3y + 5$

$3y = x - 5$

$y = \dfrac{x - 5}{3}$

$f^{-1}(x) = \dfrac{x - 5}{3}$

Example 2: Find the inverse of $f(x) = 3 - x^2$.

Answer:

Step #1: Set $y = 2 - x^2$

Step #2: Interchange x and y to get $x = 2 - y^2$

Step #3: Solve for y to get $f^{-1}(x)$.

$x = 2 - y^2$

$y^2 = -x + 2$

$y = \sqrt{-x + 2}$

$f^{-1}(x) = \sqrt{-x + 2}$ OR $f^{-1}(x) = \sqrt{2 - x}$

Example 3: Find the inverse of $f(x) = \dfrac{1}{2}x^3$.

Answer:

Step #1: Set $y = \dfrac{1}{2}x^3$

Step #2: Interchange x and y to get $x = \dfrac{1}{2}y^3$

Step #3: Solve for y to get $f^{-1}(x)$.

$$x = \dfrac{1}{2}y^3$$
$$y^3 = 2x$$
$$y = \sqrt[3]{2x}$$
$$f^{-1}(x) = \sqrt[3]{2x}$$

Example 4: Find the inverse of the function $f(x) = \sqrt{x} - 15$.

Answer:

Step #1: Set $y = \sqrt{x} - 15$

Step #2: Interchange x and y to get $x = \sqrt{y} - 15$

Step #3: Solve for y to get $f^{-1}(x)$.

$$x = \sqrt{y} - 15$$
$$\sqrt{y} = x + 15$$
$$y = (x + 15)^2$$
$$f^{-1}(x) = (x + 15)^2 \quad \text{OR} \quad f^{-1}(x) = x^2 + 30x + 225$$

Slope-Intercept Form of a Line

The most common form of equation for a line to be written in is the slope-intercept form, which is $y = mx + b$. The "*m*" in the equation represents the slope of the line, and is always just before the variable *x*. The "*b*" in the equation indicates the *y*-intercept of the equation. In other words, the "*b*" indicates where the line crosses the *y*-axis. This form is the most common because it is the simplest form to graph from.

Example of graphing using the slope-intercept form: Graph the line $y = 2x - 1$.

Answer: Because the line is in slope-intercept form (the y is alone with a coefficient of 1, and the *x* has an exponent of 1), we can we that that the slope of the line is 2 (m=2) and the *y*-intercept equals 1 (b=−1). Based on this we can plot the graph:

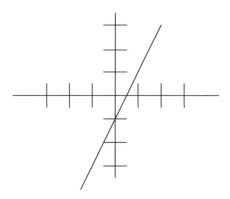

Example of writing equation in slope-intercept form: Use the following graph to write the equation of the line in slope-intercept form.

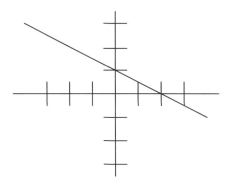

Answer: Slope-intercept form is $y = mx + b$, so we need to determine the slope "*m*" and the *y*-intercept "*b*". By looking at the graph we can clearly see that the graph intersects the *y*-axis where $y = 1$. Therefore the y-intercept, or "*b*" is 1.

To find the slope we take two arbitrary points which lie on the graph, such as (0,1) and (2,0), and use them to find slope as follows:

$$m = \frac{y_2 - y_1}{x_2 - x_1} = \frac{0 - 1}{2 - 0} = -\frac{1}{2}$$

Now, we just plug the values into the equation to find: $y = -\frac{1}{2}x + 1$

Composition of Two Functions

To find the composition of two functions means you take the function of a function. The composition of two functions takes the terms of one function and substitutes them into the other function. The composition of two functions is denoted as $f(g(x))$.

Let's say the two functions are $f(x)$ and $g(x)$. The composition of the two functions is $h(x)$.

This means $h(x) = g(f(x))$.
In other words, the composite function $h(x)$ is the function $g(x)$ of the function $f(x)$.

Note: The order of the composition matters.

$g(f(x)) \neq f(g(x))$

For example, find $g(f(x))$ and $f(g(x))$ if the functions are $f(x) = x + 4$ and $g(x) = x^2$ where x = 6.

Follow these steps to find $g(f(x))$:
Step #1: Find $f(x)$ where x = 6.

$f(6) = 6 + 4 = 10$

Step #2: Plug this answer in for $f(x)$ in $g(f(x))$.

$g(10) = 10^2 = 100$

So $g(f(x)) = 100$

Follow these steps to find $f(g(x))$:
Step #1: Find $g(x)$ where x = 6

$g(6) = 6^2 = 36$

Step #3: Plug this answer in for $g(x)$ in $f(g(x))$.

$f(36) = 36 + 4 = 40$

$f(g(x)) = 40$

As you can see $g(f(x)) \neq f(g(x))$ because $100 \neq 40$.

Example 1: Find $g(f(x))$ and $f(g(x))$ if the functions are $f(x) = \sqrt{x}$ and $g(x) = 4x^2$ where x = 9.

Answer:

Find $g(f(x))$:

$f(x) = \sqrt{9} = 3$

$g(3) = 4(3^2) = 4(9) = 36$

$g(f(x)) = 36$

Find $f(g(x))$:

$g(9) = 4(9^2) = 4(81) = 324$

$f(324) = \sqrt{324} = 18$

$f(g(x)) = 18$

Example 2: Find $g(f(x))$ and $f(g(x))$ if the functions are $f(x) = 2x + 3$ and $g(x) = 3x + 2$ where x = −1.

Answer:

Find $g(f(x))$:

$f(-1) = 2(-1) + 3 = 1$

$g(1) = 3(1) + 2 = 5$

$g(f(x)) = 5$

Find $f(g(x))$:

$g(-1) = 3(-1) + 2 = -1$

$f(-1) = 2(-1) + 3 = 1$

$f(g(x)) = 1$

Example 3: Find $g(f(x))$ and $f(g(x))$ if the functions are $f(x) = 10x + 3$ and $g(x) = \dfrac{x}{2}$ where $x = \dfrac{1}{2}$.

Answer:

Find $g(f(x))$:

$$f(\tfrac{1}{2}) = 10 \, (\tfrac{1}{2}) + 3 = 8$$

$$g(8) = \frac{8}{2} = 4$$

$$g(f(x)) = 4$$

Find $f(g(x))$:

$$g\left(\frac{1}{2}\right) = \frac{\tfrac{1}{2}}{2} = \frac{1}{4}$$

$$f\left(\frac{1}{4}\right) = 10\left(\frac{1}{4}\right) + 3 = \frac{5}{2} + 3 = \frac{11}{2} = 5.5$$

$$f(g(x)) = 5.5$$

 # Combining Functions

You can add, subtract, multiply and divide functions. To solve these types of problems, evaluate each function and then add, subtract, multiply, or divide based on the question.

Example 1: Add Functions
Given functions $f(x) = 3x$ and $g(x) = x + 5$.

Find $f(2) + g(5)$.

Answer:
Step #1: Evaluate each function.

$$f(x) = 3x$$
$$f(2) = 3(2)$$
$$f(2) = 6$$

$$g(x) = x + 5$$
$$g(5) = 5 + 5$$
$$g(5) = 10$$

Step #2: Plug in the values.

$$f(2) + g(5) = 6 + 10 = 16$$

So the answer is 16.

Example 2: Subtract Functions

Given functions $f(x) = 4x + 10$ and $g(x) = x - 4$.

Find $f(3) - g(7)$.

Answer:
Step #1: Evaluate each function.

$$f(3) = 4x + 10$$
$$f(3) = 4(3) + 10$$
$$f(3) = 22$$

$$g(x) = x - 4$$
$$g(7) = 7 - 4$$
$$g(7) = 3$$

Step #2: Plug in the values.

$$f(3) - g(7) = 22 - 3 = 19$$

So the answer is 19.

Example 3: Multiply Functions

Given functions $f(x) = x^2$ and $g(x) = x^3$.

Find $f(6) \times g(3)$.

Answer:
Step #1: Evaluate each function.

$$f(x) = x^2$$
$$f(6) = 6^2$$
$$f(6) = 36$$

$$g(x) = x^3$$
$$g(3) = 3^3$$
$$g(3) = 27$$

Step #2: Plug in the values.

$$f(6) \times g(3) = 36 \times 27 = 972$$

So the answer is 972.

Example 4: Divide Functions

Given functions $f(x) = 10x$ and $g(x) = 3x^2 + 2x - 5$.

Find $f(11) \div g(4)$.

Answer:
Step #1: Evaluate each function.

$$f(x) = 10x$$
$$f(11) = 10(11)$$
$$f(11) = 110$$

Step #2: Plug in the values.

$$f(11) \div g(4) = 110 \div 51 = \frac{110}{51} = 2.16$$

So the answer is 2.16.

Logarithms and Exponents

What are logarithms? Logarithms represent the exponent of a positive number. For example, if $b^x = N$ where "N" is a positive number and "b" is a positive number besides 1, then the exponent "x" is the logarithm of N to the base b.

This relationship can be written as $x = \log_b N$

Following are examples that will help demonstrate this relationship:

Example 1: Write $4^2 = 16$ using logarithmic notation.

2 is the logarithm of 16 to the base 4 therefore logarithmic notation is $2 = \log_4 16$

Example 2: Evaluate $\log_4 64$.

$\log_4 64$ says that you have a base = 4 and you have to figure out what x value to use in order to satisfy $4^x = 64$. Therefore, $x = 3$ and $\log_4 64 = 3$.

LAWS OF LOGARITHMS: There are 3 basic laws of logarithms which include:

1. The logarithm of the product of two positive numbers M and N is equal to the sum of the logarithms of the numbers

$$\log_b MN = \log_b M + \log_b N$$

For example, $\log_2 3(5) = \log_2 3 + \log_2 5$

2. The logarithm of the quotient of two positive numbers M and N is equal to the difference of the logarithms of the numbers

$$\log_b \frac{M}{N} = \log_b M - \log_b N$$

For example, $\log_{10} \frac{17}{24} = \log_{10} 17 - \log_{10} 24$

3. The logarithm of the "*pth*" power of a positive number *M* is equal to "*p*" multiplied by the logarithm of the number
$$\log_b M^p = p\log_b M$$

For example, $\log_8 6^4 = 4\log_8 6$

What are Natural Logarithms? Natural logarithms have a base "*e*" which is a constant. Natural logarithms are denoted by ln.

You can find "*e*" on your scientific calculator. $e = 2.718281828\ldots$

$\ln a = b$ is $e^b = a$

When would you use logarithms and exponents? Logarithms and exponents can be used when you calculate simple & compound interest and exponential growth.

Example of Simple Interest:
The formula for Simple Interest is I = Prt where I = simple interest, P = principal, r = annual interest rate, and t = time.

If you borrow $400 at 10% interest for 1 year, how much interest will you end up paying on the loan?

I = Prt
I = ($400)(0.10)(1)
I = $40 in interest
Total amount = Principle + Interest = $400 + $40 = $440

Example of Compound Interest:
Compound interest is paid periodically over the term of a loan. This gives a new principal amount at the end of <u>each</u> interval of time.

Use $A = Pe^{rt}$ when interest is compounded continuously where A = Amount of interest, P = Principal, r = annual interest rate, t = years

Find the amount of an investment if $10,000 is invested at 8% compounded continuously for 2 years.

$$A = Pe^{rt}$$
$$A = 10,000e^{(0.08)(2)}$$
$$A = \$11,735$$

Solving Exponential and Logarithmic Equations

How do you solve an exponential equation? An exponential equation is an equation that has a variable as the exponent. For example, $3^x = 15$. Because a logarithm is the opposite operation to an exponent, we can use them to solve for x.

Example 1:

$$3^x = 15$$
$$\log 3^x = \log 15$$
$$x \log 3 = \log 15$$
$$x = \frac{\log 15}{\log 3}$$
$$x \approx 2.465$$

Example 2:

$$3^{x-4} = 4^x$$
$$\log 3^{x-4} = \log 4^x$$
$$(x-4)\log 3 = x \log 4$$
$$x \log 3 - 4 \log 3 = x \log 4$$
$$x \log 3 - x \log 4 - 4 \log 3 = 0$$
$$x \log 3 - x \log 4 = 4 \log 3$$
$$x(\log 3 - \log 4) = 4 \log 3$$
$$x = \frac{4 \log 3}{\log 3 - \log 4} \approx -15.275$$

How do you solve a logarithmic equation? A logarithmic equation is solved similarly to an exponential equation. Because the two functions are opposite of each they can be used in solving. When solving an exponential equation, you take the log of both sides. When solving logarithmic equations, you do the opposite, and raise both sides to an exponent. The exponent that you use depends on the type of log. You raise it to the same base as the log so that it cancels out. For example, with the common log, it would be canceled out by being raised to base 10.

Example 1:

$$\log 3x = 2$$
$$10^{\log 3x} = 10^2$$
$$3x = 10^2$$
$$x = \frac{10^2}{3} \approx 33.3$$

Example 2:

$$\log(3x+2) = \log(x-4)$$
$$10^{\log(3x+2)} = 10^{\log(x-4)}$$
$$3x+2 = x-4$$
$$2x = -6$$
$$x = -3$$

 # Sets

What is a "set"? A set is a collection of elements. Elements can be any type of number. A finite set has a specific number of elements while an infinite set as an unlimited number of elements.

What are examples of sets? Elements of a set are placed within braces { } and each element is separated by a comma.

Example of a finite set: A = {3, 4, 5, 6, 7, 8}
This is a finite set because it has a specific number of elements. There are six elements in this set.

Example of an infinite set: W = {0, 1, 2, 3, 4, …}
The "…" denotes that the elements in the set continue on infinitely.
In this case, the set W represents all the Whole numbers.

What notation do you use with sets?
Set notation uses symbols for each definition. Following is a list of relationships between sets and their symbols.

Empty Set: An empty set is also referred to as a null set. An empty set does NOT have any elements in it and is represented by {} or ø.

 Common Mistake: It may be tempting to identify {0} as an empty set. However, {0} is not an empty set because it contains one element which is the number 0.

Union of Two Sets: A union of two sets means that you combine the elements of one set with the elements of the other set to create one, larger set. A union of two sets is denoted by ∪.
 Example: Let's say you have two sets, set A and set B.
 A = {1, 2, 3, 4} and B = {2, 4, 6, 8}.
 A∪B = {1, 2, 3, 4, 6, 8}

 Note: You don't write the numbers A and B have in common twice. For example, both A and B had "2" and "4" in common. You only write "2" and "4" ONCE in the union of sets A and B.

Intersection of Two Sets: An intersection of two sets means that you only write the elements that are common to both sets. An intersection of two sets is denoted by ∩.

 Example: Let's say you have two sets, set C and set D.
 C = {2, 3, 4, 5, 6, 7, 8} and D = {6, 7, 8, 9}.
 C∩D = {6, 7, 8} because these are the only numbers that are in both set C and set D.

 Note: What if the two sets have no elements in common? For example, what if you had A = {1, 3, 5} and B = {2, 4, 6, 8}? They don't have any numbers in common. In this case, the two sets are disjoint and you write their intersection as the empty set {}.

Subset: The ⊂ symbol is used to denote a subset. A ⊂ B means that A is a subset of B.
 Example of a Subset: A = {1, 2, 3} and B = {1, 2, 3, 4, 5, 6}
 Every number in set A is in set B therefore, A is a subset of B, A ⊂ B.

However, B is NOT a subset of A. Why not? $B \not\subset A$ because set B has more elements than set A and therefore can't be a subset of set A.

Real Number System

What is the real number system? The real number system consists of many different types of numbers including:
- Natural numbers
- Whole numbers
- Integers
- Rational numbers
- Irrational numbers

Natural Numbers include $\{1, 2, 3, 4, 5,...\}$

Whole Numbers include $\{0, 1, 2, 3, 4, 5,...\}$

Integers include $\{..., -4, -3, -2, -1, 0, 1, 2, 3, 4,...\}$

Rational Numbers: Rational numbers are numbers that can be expressed as a fraction. The fraction can be proper or improper and positive or negative. Examples include:

$$\frac{7}{11}, \frac{7}{-11}, \frac{9}{8}, \frac{9}{-8}$$

Irrational Numbers: Numbers that can't be expressed as a fraction. Irrational numbers include numbers decimals that continue on forever such as π. If a number is not rational then it is irrational.

What are Complex numbers? Complex numbers involve imaginary numbers. Imaginary numbers are represented by i. An imaginary number would be used when you are trying to find square root of a negative number. (i.e. $\sqrt{-4}$).

Here's how it works:

$\sqrt{-4}$
$(\sqrt{4})(\sqrt{-1})$
$i\sqrt{4}$
$2i$

You will need to memorize the following regarding imaginary numbers:

$$i = \sqrt{-1} \qquad i^2 = -1 \qquad i^3 = -i \quad i^4 = 1 \qquad i^5 = i$$

A complex number is written in the form a + bi where "a" and "b" are real numbers and $i = \sqrt{-1}$. "a" is referred to as the real part of the number and "b" is referred to as the imaginary part of the number.

How do you work with Complex numbers? Follow these rules for complex numbers regarding each basic operation.

1. ADDITION OF COMPLEX NUMBERS:
   Add the "real" parts and "imaginary" parts separately.

   For example,
   $(3 + 4i) + (7 + 12i) = (3+7) + (4+12)i = 10 + 16i$

2. SUBTRACTION OF COMPLEX NUMBERS:
   Subtract the "real" parts and "imaginary" parts separately.

   For example,
   $(3 + 4i) - (7 + 12i) = (3-7) + (4-12)i = -4 - 8i$

3. MULTIPLICATION OF COMPLEX NUMBERS:
   Multiply the terms by using the FOIL method and replace i^2 with a -1.

   For example,
   $(5 + 3i)(2 - 2i) = 10 - 10i + 6i - 6i^2 = 10 - 4i - 6(-1) = \mathbf{16 - 4i}$

4. DIVISION OF COMPLEX NUMBERS:
   Multiply the numerator and denominator of the fraction by the conjugate of the denominator. Note: The conjugate of a + bi is a − bi.

   For example,

   $$\frac{2+i}{3-4i} = \frac{2+i}{3-4i} \times \frac{3+4i}{3+4i} = \frac{6+11i+4i^2}{9-16i^2} = \frac{2+11i}{25}$$

What is the "conjugate" of a complex number? The conjugate of $a + bi$ is $a - bi$ and vice versa.

> **Question:** What is the conjugate of $5 - 3i$?
> **Answer:** $5 + 3i$

Sequences and Series

What is a sequence? A sequence of numbers is a function defined on the set of positive integers. The numbers in the sequence are called "terms".

> **Arithmetic Sequences:** An arithmetic sequence is a sequence of numbers that are determined by adding a constant to the preceding number. For example: 4, 8, 12, 16…is an arithmetic sequence.

> **Geometric Sequences:** A geometric sequence is a sequence of numbers that are obtained by multiplying a constant by the preceding number. For example, 5, 10, 20, 40, 80…is a geometric sequence.

What is a series? A series is the sum of the terms of a sequence.

> **Infinite Geometric Series:** The sum to infinity ($S\infty$) of any geometric sequence in which the multiplied constant "r" is numerically less than 1 is given by:

$$S\infty = \frac{a}{1-r}, where |r| < 1 \text{ and } a = \text{the first number in the series.}$$

For example, $1 - \frac{1}{2} + \frac{1}{4} - \frac{1}{8} + ...$ where $r = -\frac{1}{2}$ because each successive term in the series is equal to the previous term multiplied by $-\frac{1}{2}$.

$$S\infty = \frac{a}{1-r} = \frac{1}{1-(-1/2)} = \frac{1}{3/2} = \frac{2}{3}$$

Factorials

What is a factorial? A factorial is denoted by the ! symbol, and is defined as $n! = n(n-1)(n-2)(n-3)...(1)$ where n is any natural number.

For example,

$$3! = 3 \cdot 2 \cdot 1 = 6$$
$$4! = 4 \cdot 3 \cdot 2 \cdot 1 = 24$$
$$5! = 5 \cdot 4 \cdot 3 \cdot 2 \cdot 1 = 120$$

Some properties of factorials that you need to remember are

$$0! = 1$$

and

$$n(n-1)! = n!$$

For example,

$$5(4!)$$
$$= 5(5-1)!$$
$$-5(4 \cdot 3 \cdot 2 \cdot 1) = 5!$$

Binomial Theorem

What is the Binomial Theorem? Essentially, the binomial theorem is a method of expanding polynomials (specifically binomials) of the form $(a+b)$ (or another two variables) which are to an exponent. The binomial theorem states that if n is any positive number then:

$$(a+b)^n = a^n + \frac{n!}{1!(n-1)!}a^{n-1}b + \frac{n!}{2!(n-2)!}a^{n-2}b^2 + \frac{n!}{3!(n-3)!}a^{n-3}b^3 + \dots + b^n$$

Example:

$$(a+b)^3 = a^3 + \frac{3!}{1!(3-1)!}a^{3-1}b + \frac{3!}{2!(3-2)!}a^{3-2}b^2 + b^3$$
$$(a+b)^3 = a^3 + \frac{3!}{1!(2)!}a^2b + \frac{3!}{2!(1)!}a^1b^2 + b^3$$
$$(a+b)^3 = a^3 + 3a^2b + 3a^1b^2 + b^3$$

Hint: Essentially, for one variable the exponents increase by one per term, starting at zero, and goes until it reaches the designated exponent. For the other it decreases by one per term, starting at the designated exponent and moving to zero.

 # Determinants of 2 x 2 Matrices

How do you find the determinant of a 2x2 matrix? If a, b, c, and d are numbers, the determinant of matrix $A = \begin{bmatrix} a & b \\ c & d \end{bmatrix}$ is:

$$A = \begin{bmatrix} a & b \\ c & d \end{bmatrix}$$

$$\det(A) = ad - bc$$

Example:

$$B = \begin{bmatrix} 2 & 5 \\ 1 & 6 \end{bmatrix}$$

$$\det(B) = 2(6) - 1(6) = 12 - 6 = 6$$

$$C = \begin{bmatrix} 2 & 5 \\ 1 & -6 \end{bmatrix}$$

$$\det(C) = 2(-6) - 1(5) = -12 - 5 = -17$$

 # Finding Slopes

The slope of a line is the ratio of change along the vertical to the change along the horizontal. In other words, the steepness of the line.

The Slope Formula states: The slope, m, of the line that contains the points (x_1, y_1)

and (x_2, y_2) is given by: $m = \dfrac{y_2 - y_1}{x_2 - x_1} = \dfrac{rise}{run}$

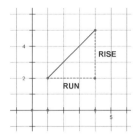

Example 1: Find the slope of a line that contains points (2,5) and (6,11).

$$m = \frac{11-5}{6-2} = \frac{6}{4} = \frac{3}{2}$$

Example 2: Find the slope of a line that contains points (18,4) and (3,14).

$$m = \frac{14-4}{3-18} = \frac{10}{-15} = \frac{-2}{3}$$

5 Tips about Slope:

Tip #1: Notice that the slope of Example 1, $\frac{3}{2}$ and the slope of Example 2, $\frac{-2}{3}$ are the negative reciprocal of each other. This means the lines are perpendicular to each other.

Tip #2: In contrast, parallel lines have the same slope.

Tip #3: A horizontal line has a slope of zero. (It remains flat.)

Tip #4: A vertical line has an undefined slope. (The difference between the x-values is zero and a fraction with a zero denominator is undefined.)

Tip #5: Always write slope in its simplest form. For example, $\frac{4}{8}$ should be written as $\frac{1}{2}$.

Sample Problems on Slope

1. Find the slope of a line with points (3,7) and (21, 15).

Answer: $m = \dfrac{15-7}{21-3} = \dfrac{8}{18} = \dfrac{4}{9}$

2. Find the slope of a line with points (3,4) and (3,10).

Answer: $m = \dfrac{10-4}{3-3} = \dfrac{6}{0} =$ undefined slope

3. Find the slope of a line with points $\left(\dfrac{1}{2}, \dfrac{3}{4}\right)$ and $\left(\dfrac{3}{2}, \dfrac{1}{4}\right)$.

Answer: $m = \dfrac{\left(\dfrac{1}{4} - \dfrac{3}{4}\right)}{\left(\dfrac{3}{2} - \dfrac{1}{2}\right)} = \dfrac{\dfrac{-2}{4}}{\dfrac{2}{2}} = \dfrac{\dfrac{-1}{2}}{1} = \dfrac{-1}{2}$

4. Find the slope of a line with points (15,6) and (21,6).

Answer: $m = \dfrac{6-6}{21-15} = \dfrac{0}{6} = 0$

5. Find the slope of the line in the graph below:

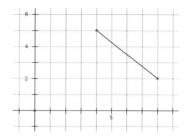

Answer: $\dfrac{Rise}{Run} = \dfrac{-3 \ units}{4 \ units} = \dfrac{-3}{4}$

🎓 *Finding Intercepts*

X-intercept:
The x-intercept is the point at which a graph of an equation crosses the x-axis.

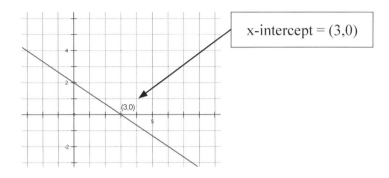

To find the x-intercept set y = 0 and solve for x in the linear equation.

Example: Find the x-intercept of the linear equation $2x + 3y = 6$.

Answer: Set y = 0 and solve for x.

$2x + 3y = 6$
$2x + 3(0) = 6$
$2x = 6$
$x = 3$

So the x-intercept is (3,0).

Note: If you are given just the graph look for the point that crosses the x-axis as shown above.

Y-intercept:
The y-intercept is the point at which a graph crosses the y-axis.

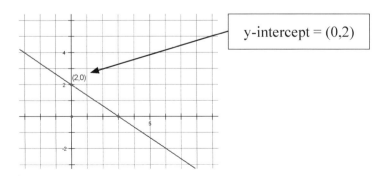

To find the y-intercept set x = 0 and solve for y in the linear equation.

Example: Find the y-intercept of the linear equation $2x + 3y = 6$.

Answer: Set x = 0 and solve for y.

$2x + 3y = 6$
$2(0) + 3y = 6$
$3y = 6$
$y = 2$

So the y-intercept is (0,2).

Note: If you are given just the graph look for the point that crosses the y-axis as shown above.

Example 1: Find the x and y intercepts of the following graph.

Answer: Find the coordinates where the line crosses the x and y-axes.
x-intercept = (−1,0)
y-intercept = (0,4)

Example 2: Find the x and y-intercepts of the equation $12x + 6y = 60$.

Answer:
Find x-intercept by setting y = 0 and solving for x.

$12x + 6y = 60$
$12x + 6(0) = 60$
$12x = 60$
$x = 5$

So the x-intercept is (5,0).

Find y-intercept by setting x = 0 and solving for y.

$$12x + 6y = 60$$
$$12(0) + 6y = 60$$
$$6y = 60$$
$$y = 10$$

So the y-intercept is (0,10).

Example 3: Find the x and y intercepts of the equation $4x = 28$.
Find the x-intercept by setting y = 0 and solving for x.

There is no "y" in the equation.

$$4x = 28$$
$$x = 7$$

So the x-intercept is (7,0).

There is no y-intercept because 4x = 28 is a vertical line. X is the same value for every value of y. The graph below demonstrates this concept.

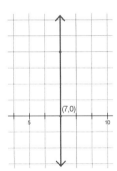

Example 4: Find the x and y intercepts of the equation $10y = 20$.
There is no "x" in the equation so there is no x-intercept.

Find the y-intercept by solving for y.

$$10y = 20$$
$$y = 2$$

So the y-intercept is (0,2).

There is no x-intercept because 10y = 20 is a horizontal line. Y is the same value for every value of x. The graph below demonstrates this concept.

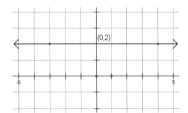

 # *Operations with Matrices*

A matrix is a rectangular table of numbers that are arranged in m horizontal rows and n vertical columns. The numbers in the matrix are called the "elements". The matrix is denoted as m x n or "m by n".

Matrix "A" is shown below:

$$A = \begin{bmatrix} 4 & 7 & -1 \\ 2 & -3 & 5 \\ 1 & 6 & 8 \\ 3 & -2 & -4 \end{bmatrix}$$ Matrix "A" is a 4 x 3 matrix. So its dimension is 4 x 3.

Elements in a matrix are referred to by the row number and then the column number.

Example: $a_{13} = -1$ because the number in the first row, third column is −1.

Matrix Addition and Subtraction: To add and subtract matrices, each matrix must have the same dimension.

Example of Matrix Addition: $\begin{bmatrix} 2 & -1 \\ 4 & 3 \end{bmatrix} + \begin{bmatrix} -3 & 7 \\ 2 & 5 \end{bmatrix} = ?$

Answer: Add corresponding pairs of elements.

$$\begin{bmatrix} 2 & -1 \\ 4 & 3 \end{bmatrix} + \begin{bmatrix} -3 & 7 \\ 2 & 5 \end{bmatrix} = \begin{bmatrix} 2+(-3) & -1+7 \\ 4+2 & 3+5 \end{bmatrix} = \begin{bmatrix} -1 & 6 \\ 6 & 8 \end{bmatrix}$$

Example of Matrix Subtraction: $\begin{bmatrix} 2 & -1 \\ 4 & 3 \end{bmatrix} - \begin{bmatrix} -3 & 7 \\ 2 & 5 \end{bmatrix} = ?$

Answer: Subtract corresponding pairs of elements.

$$\begin{bmatrix} 2 & -1 \\ 4 & 3 \end{bmatrix} - \begin{bmatrix} -3 & 7 \\ 2 & 5 \end{bmatrix} = \begin{bmatrix} 2-(-3) & -1-7 \\ 4-2 & 3-5 \end{bmatrix} = \begin{bmatrix} 5 & -8 \\ 2 & -2 \end{bmatrix}$$

Matrix Multiplication:

Example of Scalar Multiplication: $3\begin{bmatrix} 2 & -1 \\ 4 & 3 \end{bmatrix} = ?$

Answer: Multiply 3 by each element.

$$3\begin{bmatrix} 2 & -1 \\ 4 & 3 \end{bmatrix} = \begin{bmatrix} 3(2) & 3(-1) \\ 3(4) & 3(3) \end{bmatrix} = \begin{bmatrix} 6 & -3 \\ 12 & 9 \end{bmatrix}$$

Example of Column Multiplication: $\begin{bmatrix} 2 & 5 & -1 \end{bmatrix}\begin{bmatrix} 3 \\ -4 \\ 7 \end{bmatrix} = ?$

Answer: Multiply the first element in the row by the first element in the column, the second element in the row by the second element in the column, and the third element in the row by the third element in the column. Find the sum of these products.

$$\begin{bmatrix} 2 & 5 & -1 \end{bmatrix}\begin{bmatrix} 3 \\ -4 \\ 7 \end{bmatrix} = \begin{bmatrix} 2\cdot3 + 5\cdot(-4) + (-1)\cdot7 \end{bmatrix} = [6 + (-20) + (-7)] = \begin{bmatrix} -21 \end{bmatrix}$$

Example of Matrix Multiplication: $AB = \begin{bmatrix} 2 & 5 & -1 \\ 3 & 1 & 6 \end{bmatrix}\begin{bmatrix} 4 & 2 \\ 1 & 7 \\ 8 & 4 \end{bmatrix} = ?$

Answer: Multiply the ith row of matrix A by the jth column of matrix B.

$$AB = \begin{bmatrix} 2 & 5 & -1 \\ 3 & 1 & 6 \end{bmatrix}\begin{bmatrix} 4 & 2 \\ 1 & 7 \\ 8 & 4 \end{bmatrix} = \begin{bmatrix} 2(4)+5(1)+(-1)(8) & 2(2)+5(7)+(-1)(4) \\ 3(4)+1(1)+6(8) & 3(2)+1(7)+6(4) \end{bmatrix} = \begin{bmatrix} 5 & 35 \\ 61 & 37 \end{bmatrix}$$

Methods of Solving Two and Three Variable Systems

You can solve systems of equations graphically or algebraically.
Note: The solutions of two variable systems include no solutions, one solution, and infinite solutions.

Linear equations that do not intersect have no solution.
Linear equations that intersect at one point have one solution.
Linear equations that are the same equation written in different forms have infinite solutions. (The graphs lie on top of each other.)

Example 1 of Two Variable Systems: Solve the system of equations $\begin{cases} x + y = 5 \\ 4x - 2y = 2 \end{cases}$

Method #1: Solve the system of equations graphically.
Graph each linear equation. The intersection of the lines is the solution of the equation.

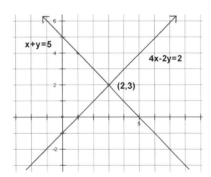

The solution of the system is x = 2 and y = 3 because the graphs intersect at (2,3).

Method #2: Solve the system of equations algebraically.

One way to use algebra is to use the elimination method. Cancel out the y variable to allow you to solve for the x variable.

Given:

$x + y = 5$
$4x - 2y = 2$

Multiply the first equation by 2 so you can eliminate the y-variable.

$2(x + y = 5)$
$2x + 2y = 10$

Add the two equations and solve for x. (This will enable you to eliminate the y-variable.)

$$2x + 2y = 10$$
$$\underline{4x - 2y = 2}$$
$$6x = 12$$
$$x = 2$$

Next plug in the value x = 2 to solve for y. You can plug it into either equation.

$x + y = 5$
$2 + y = 5$
$y = 3$

So the solution to the two equations is (2,3).

Example 2 of Two Variable Systems: Solve the system of equations $\begin{cases} 2x + y = 10 \\ x + 4y = 12 \end{cases}$

Method #1: Solve the system of equations graphically.
Graph each linear equation. The intersection of each equation is the solution of the equation.

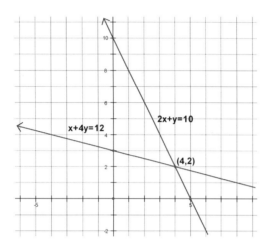

The solution of the system is x = 4 and y = 2 because the graphs intersect at (4,2).

Method #2: Solve the system of equations algebraically.

One way to use algebra is to use the elimination method. Cancel out the y variable to allow you to solve for the x variable.

Given:

$2x + y = 10$
$x + 4y = 12$

Multiply the first equation by –4 so you can eliminate the y-variable.

$-4(2x + y = 10)$
$-8x - 4y = -40$

Add the two equations and solve for x. (This will enable you to eliminate the y-variable.)

$$-8x - 4y = -40$$
$$\underline{x + 4y = 12}$$
$$-7x = -28$$
$$x = 4$$

Next plug in the value x = 4 to solve for y. You can plug it into either equation.

$$2x + y = 10$$
$$2(4) + y = 10$$
$$8 + y = 10$$
$$y = 2$$

So the solution to the two equations is (4,2).

Solving Three Variable Systems:
Three variable systems are systems of planes. You can solve them graphically or algebraically.

Solutions of systems of three variables include no solution, one solution, or infinite solutions. All three planes must intersect at the same point to have one solution.

Example of Three Variable Systems:

Solve the following three variable system using the elimination method:

$$\begin{cases} x - y + 2z = 14 & \text{(A)} \\ 2x + y + 3z = 28 & \text{(B)} \\ x - y + z = 8 & \text{(C)} \end{cases}$$

Step #1: Pair equations to eliminate one variable.

$$(A) x - y + 2z = 14$$
$$\underline{(B) 2x + y + 3z = 28}$$
$$(E) 3x + 5z = 42$$

AND

$(B) 2x + y + 3z = 28$

$(C) x - y + z = 8$

$(F) 3x + 4z = 36$

Step #2: Solve the new system.

$(E) 3x + 5z = 42$

$(F) 3x + 4z = 36$

Multiply -1 by (F) to eliminate the x variable.

$(E) 3x + 5z = 42$

$(F) -3x - 4z = -36$

$z = 6$

Step #3: Plug $z = 6$ into (E) to solve for x.

$(E) 3x + 5z = 42$

$3x + 5(6) = 42$

$3x = 12$

$x = 4$

Step #4: Plug $x = 4$ and $z = 6$ into (A) to find y.

$(A) x - y + 2z = 14$

$4 - y + 2(6) = 14$

$-y = -2$

$y = 2$

So the solution (x, y, z) is (4, 2, 6).

Exponential and Radical Expressions

Use the "Rules of Exponents" to evaluate exponential expressions. In order to use these rules each term **MUST** have the **SAME** Variable.

Basic rules of exponents:

I. Negative Integral Exponent:

If n is a positive integer and $a^n \neq 0$, then $a^{-n} = \dfrac{1}{a^n}$.

Example: 2^{-5} can be written as $\dfrac{1}{2^5}$.

Always write your final answer in terms of a positive exponent.

II. Product Rule: When multiplying two terms, just **ADD** their exponents and **MULTIPLY** their coefficients.

Example with positive exponents:
$4x^5 \times 2x^2$
Answer: $(4 \times 2)(x^{5+2}) = 8x^7$

Example with negative exponents:
$3x^2 \times 2x^{-4}$

Answer: $(3 \times 2)(x^{2+(-4)}) = 6x^{-2} = \dfrac{6}{x^2}$

Note: The number "6" stays in the numerator because it has its own exponent of "1" which is already positive.

Example with fractional exponents:
$x^{\frac{1}{2}} \times 2x^{\frac{3}{4}}$
Answer: $(1 \times 2)(x^{\frac{1}{2}+\frac{3}{4}}) = 2x^{\frac{5}{4}}$

III. Quotient Rule: When dividing two terms, just **SUBTRACT** their exponents and **DIVIDE** their coefficients.
Note: You MUST subtract the bottom exponent from the top exponent.

Example with positive exponents:

$$\frac{15y^8}{5y^2}$$

Answer: $\frac{15y^8}{5y^2} = \frac{15}{3}(y^{8-2}) = 3y^6$

Example with negative exponents:

$$\frac{20y^3}{10y^9}$$

Answer: $\frac{20y^3}{10y^9} = 2(y^{3-9}) = 2y^{-6} = \frac{2}{y^6}$

Example with fractional exponents:

$$\frac{3y^{\frac{2}{3}}}{9y^{\frac{1}{3}}}$$

Answer: $\frac{3y^{\frac{2}{3}}}{9y^{\frac{1}{3}}} = \frac{1}{3}(y^{\frac{2}{3}-\frac{1}{3}}) = \frac{1}{3}y^{\frac{1}{3}}$

IV. Power Rule: Use this rule when a term is inside parentheses AND raised to a power. In this case you would **MULTIPLY** the exponents and coefficients by the power on the outside of the parentheses.

Example with positive exponents:

$(3x^7)^3$

Answer: $(3)^3(x^7)^3 = 27x^{21}$

Example with negative exponents:

$(2x^4)^{-5}$

Answer: $(2)^{-5}(x^4)^{-5} = 2^{-5}x^{-20} = \dfrac{1}{2^5}\left(\dfrac{1}{x^{20}}\right) = \dfrac{1}{32x^{20}}$

Example with fractional exponents:

$(25x^4)^{\frac{1}{2}}$

Answer: $(25)^{\frac{1}{2}}(x^4)^{\frac{1}{2}} = 25^{\frac{1}{2}}\left(x^{4\times\frac{1}{2}}\right) = 5x^2$

Radical Expressions:

A radical expression has the form $\sqrt[n]{a}$.

Note: When n = 2 you do not need to write it, just use the $\sqrt{}$ sign.

Example: $\sqrt[3]{8}$ has n = 3 and a = 8.

To evaluate $\sqrt[3]{8}$ you find the 3rd root of 8. In other words, what number times itself times itself again equals 8? The answer is 2 because 2 x 2 x 2 = 8.

Note: $\sqrt[3]{8}$ can be written as $8^{\frac{1}{3}}$.

Laws for Radical Expressions: The laws for radical expressions are the same as the laws used in exponents.

I. $\left(\sqrt[n]{a}\right)^n = a$

Example:

$\left(\sqrt[4]{8}\right)^4$

Answer: $\left(\sqrt[4]{8}\right)^4 = \left(8^{\frac{1}{4}}\right)^4 = 8^{\frac{1}{4}\times 4} = 8^1 = 8$

II. $\sqrt[n]{ab} = \sqrt[n]{a}\sqrt[n]{b}$

Example:

$\sqrt[3]{16}$

Answer: $\sqrt[3]{16} = \sqrt[3]{8 \cdot 2} = \sqrt[3]{8} \cdot \sqrt[3]{2} = 2\sqrt[3]{2}$

III. $\sqrt[n]{\dfrac{a}{b}} = \dfrac{\sqrt[n]{a}}{\sqrt[n]{b}}$ where $b \neq 0$

Example:

$\sqrt[3]{\dfrac{10}{27}}$

Answer: $\sqrt[3]{\dfrac{10}{27}} = \dfrac{\sqrt[3]{10}}{\sqrt[3]{27}} = \dfrac{\sqrt[3]{10}}{3}$

IV. $\sqrt[n]{a^m} = \left(\sqrt[n]{a}\right)^m$

Example:

$\sqrt[3]{8^4}$

Answer: $\sqrt[3]{8^4} = \left(\sqrt[3]{8}\right)^4 = 2^4 = 16$

V. $\sqrt[m]{\sqrt[n]{a}} = \sqrt[mn]{a}$

Example:

$\sqrt[5]{\sqrt[2]{6}}$

Answer: $\sqrt[5]{\sqrt[2]{6}} = \sqrt[10]{6}$

Two Dimensional Graphing

You can graph linear equations by finding at least three coordinates that satisfy the equation.

Example 1: Draw the graph of the equation $2x + 4y = 16$

Find the x-intercept and y-intercept.

x-intercept:

$$2x + 4y = 16$$
$$2x + 4(0) = 16$$
$$2x = 16$$
$$x = 8$$

So the x-intercept is (8,0).

y-intercept:

$$2x + 4y = 16$$
$$2(0) + 4y = 16$$
$$4y = 16$$
$$y = 4$$

So the y-intercept is (0,4).

An easy way to find a third point on the graph is to write the equation in terms of y.

$$2x + 4y = 16$$
$$4y = 16 - 2x$$
$$y = 4 - \frac{1}{2}x$$

Then pick an arbitrary value for x. Then solve for y. Let's say x = 4, then solve for y.

$$y = 4 - \frac{1}{2}x$$

$$y = 4 - \frac{1}{2}(4)$$

$$y = 4 - 2 = 2$$

So (4,2)

Create a table to organize the three points (x, y) that satisfy the equation.

x	y	(x,y)
0	4	(0, 4)
8	0	(8,0)
4	2	(4,2)

Graph the three points and draw a line through the points.

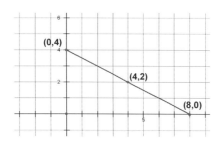

Example 2: Draw the graph of the equation 5x + 2y = 20

Find the x-intercept and y-intercept.

x-intercept:

$$5x + 2y = 20$$
$$5x + 2(0) = 20$$
$$5x = 20$$
$$x = 4$$

So the x-intercept is (4,0).

y-intercept:

$$5x + 2y = 20$$
$$5(0) + 2y = 20$$
$$2y = 20$$
$$y = 10$$

So the y-intercept is (0,10).

An easy way to find a third point on the graph is to write the equation in terms of y.

Sample Test Questions

SECTION 1: ALGEBRAIC OPERATIONS

1. Factor $x^2 - 3x - 28$

   A. $(x+3)(x+8)$

   B. $(x+4)(x-7)$

   C. $(x+4)(x+7)$

   D. $(x-4)(x+7)$

   E. $(x-4)(x-7)$

2. Factor $x^2 - 25$

   A. $(x^2+5)^2$

   B. $(x^2-5)^2$

   C. $(x-5)(x-5)$

   D. $(x+5)(x-5)$

   E. $(x+5)(x+5)$

3. Factor $w^2 + 2wx + x^2$

   A. $(w+x)^2$

   B. $w(w-x^2)$

   C. $(w-x)(w-x)$

   D. $(w-x)(w+x)$

   E. $(w-x)^2$

4. Expand $(x+3)^2$

   A. $x^2 + 3x + 9$

   B. $x^2 + 9x + 3$

   C. $x^2 + 6x + 9$

   D. $x^2 + 9x + 6$

   E. $x^2 + 3x + 6$

5. Expand $(x+3)(x-2)$

   A. $x^2 - 5x + 6$

   B. $x^2 + 5x + 6$

   C. $x^2 - x + 6$

   D. $x^2 + x + 6$

   E. $x^2 + x - 6$

6. Expand $(x^2 + 2)(x - 2)$

   A. $x^3 - 2x^2 + 2x - 4$

   B. $x^3 + 2x^2 + 2x - 4$

   C. $x^3 + 2x^2 + 2x + 4$

   D. $x^3 + 2x^2 - 2x + 4$

   E. $x^3 - 2x^2 - 2x - 4$

7. Add $(x^2 + 2x - 3) + (x^2 + 4x + 14)$

   A. $(2x^2 + 6x + 11)$

   B. $(2x^2 + 6x - 11)$

   C. $(x^2 + 6x + 11)$

   D. $(x^2 + 6x + 17)$

   E. $(2x^2 + 6x + 17)$

8. Subtract $(3x^2 - 2x + 7) - (4x^2 + x - 3)$

   A. $7x^2 - 3x + 10$

   B. $7x^2 - x + 4$

   C. $-x^2 - 3x + 1($

   D. $-x^2 - 3x + 10$

   E. $-x^2 + x + 10$

9. Simplify $\dfrac{x^2+5x+6}{x^2+7x+12}$

    A. $\dfrac{x+4}{x+3}$

    B. $\dfrac{x+2}{x+3}$

    C. $\dfrac{x+2}{x+4}$

    D. $\dfrac{x+2}{x+3}$

    E. $x^2+\dfrac{5}{7}x+\dfrac{1}{2}$

10. Add $(x^2+\dfrac{1}{2}x+\dfrac{1}{2})+(2x^2+\dfrac{1}{2}x+\dfrac{1}{2})$

    A. x^2+x+1

    B. $3x^2+x+1$

    C. $x^2+\dfrac{1}{2}x+1$

    D. $x^2+\dfrac{1}{2}x+\dfrac{1}{2}$

    E. $2x^2+\dfrac{1}{2}x+\dfrac{1}{2}$

11. Subtract $(x^2-\dfrac{3}{4}x+2)-(2x^2-\dfrac{1}{4}x-1)$

    A. $x^2-\dfrac{1}{2}x+1$

    B. $-x^2-\dfrac{1}{2}x+1$

    C. $-x^2-x+3$

    D. $x^2-\dfrac{1}{2}x+3$

    E. $-x^2-\dfrac{1}{2}x+3$

12. Multiply $(x+7)(3-x)$

    A. $-x^2-4x+21$

    B. $x^2-4x+21$

    C. $x^2+4x+21$

    D. $-x^2+4x+21$

    E. $-x^2+10x+21$

13. Multiply $x^5 \cdot x^2$

    A. x^{23}

    B. x^{10}

    C. x^7

    D. x^3

    E. Operation cannot be performed

14. Divide $\dfrac{x^3}{x^2}$

    A. $\dfrac{x^2}{x^3}$

    B. $\dfrac{1}{x}$

    C. $x^{\frac{2}{3}}$

    D. x

    E. None of the above

15. Simplify $\dfrac{x^2 - x - 2}{x + 1}$

    A. $\dfrac{x-2}{x+1}$

    B. $x - 2$

    C. $\dfrac{x+1}{x-2}$

    D. $\dfrac{x-2}{x+2}$

    E. $x + 1$

16. Simplify $\dfrac{x^2 + 9}{x - 3}$

    A. $\dfrac{x-9}{x+3}$

    B. $x + 3$

    C. $x + 9$

    D. $\dfrac{1}{x-3}$

    E. Cannot be simplified further

17. Simplify $(x^3)^2$

    A. x^6

    B. x^9

    C. x^5

    D. $x^{\frac{1}{2}}$

    E. x^1

18. Rewrite in exponential form $\log_9 81 = 2$

    A. $81^{\frac{1}{2}} = 9$

    B. $2^9 = 81$

    C. $9^2 = 81$

    D. $81^{\frac{1}{9}} = 2$

    E. $9(2) = 18$

19. Rewrite in exponential form $\log_7 x = 3$

    A. $7^x = 3$

    B. $7^3 = x$

    C. $x^7 = 3$

    D. $x^3 = 7$

    E. $3^7 = x$

20. Rewrite in logarithmic form $6^2 = 36$

    A. $\log_{36} 36 = 6$

    B. $\log_{36} 2 = 36$

    C. $\log_2 6 = 36$

    D. $\log_2 36 = 6$

    E. $\log_6 36 = 2$

21. Rewrite in exponential form $\log 100 = x$

    A. $10^x = 100$

    B. $10^{100} = x$

    C. $100 = x$

    D. $100^x = 10$

    E. $x = 0$

22. Simplify $\log_6 x - \log_6 y$

    A. $\log_6 \dfrac{x}{y}$

    B. $\log_6 \dfrac{y}{x}$

    C. $\log_6 xy$

    D. $\log_6 (x+y)$

    E. $\log_6 (x-y)$

23. Simplify $\log x + \log y - \log z$

    A. $\log x(y-z)$

    B. $\log xyz$

    C. $\log \dfrac{xz}{y}$

    D. $\log \dfrac{xy}{z}$

    E. $\log \dfrac{x}{yz}$

24. Expand $\log \dfrac{x^2 y}{z}$

    A. $\log x + \log y + \log z$

    B. $\log x + \log y - \log z$

    C. $2\log x + \log y - \log z$

    D. $2\log x + \log y + \log z$

    E. $2\log x - \log y + \log z$

25. Expand $\ln \dfrac{x+3}{yz}$

    A. $\ln(x+3) - \ln y + \ln z$

    B. $\ln(x+3) - (\ln y + \ln z)$

    C. $\ln x + 3 - \ln y + \ln z$

    D. $\ln x + \ln 3 - \ln y + \ln z$

    E. $\ln(x+3) + \ln y + \ln z$

SECTION 2: EQUATIONS AND INEQUALITIES

1. $\dfrac{4}{5}x + 19 = x - 1$

   $x = ?$

   A. 20
   B. 5
   C. 4
   D. 13
   E. 100

2. $x^2 - 7x = -12$

   $x = ?$

   A. 0
   B. 3
   C. 4 and 0
   D. 3 and 4
   E. Cannot be solved

3. Solve $x^2 > 25$

   A. $x > 5$
   B. $x \leq 5$
   C. $x > 25$
   D. $x \leq -25$
   E. $x < 5$

4. Solve $-\dfrac{x}{2} + 7 \leq 14$

   A. $x > 14$
   B. $x \geq 14$
   C. $x \geq -14$
   D. $x \leq -14$
   E. $x = -14$

5. Solve $-x = 17 - 21x$

    A. $x = \dfrac{20}{17}$

    B. $x = \dfrac{17}{20}$

    C. $x = 20$

    D. $x = 17$

    E. $x = \dfrac{7}{20}$

6. Solve $x - 12 = \dfrac{1}{2}x + 7$

    A. $x = 17$

    B. $x = 39$

    C. $x = 38$

    D. $x = 19$

    E. Cannot be solved

7. Find the roots of $y = x^2 - 15x + 50$

    A. 0 and 3

    B. 0 and 5

    C. 5 and 10

    D. 10 and 3

    E. 10 and 0

8. Find the roots of $y = x^2 - 8x + 12$

    A. 0 and 2

    B. 0 and –2

    C. –2 and 6

    D. 2 and 6

    E. 2 and –3

9. Find the roots of $y = x^2 + 12x + 2$

   A. $-6 \pm \dfrac{\sqrt{136}}{2}$

   B. -6 and -2

   C. 6 and 2

   D. $-6 \pm \dfrac{\sqrt{136}}{4}$

   E. Imaginary answer

10. Find the roots of $y = x^2 + 2x + 2$

   A. $-6 \pm \dfrac{\sqrt{136}}{2}$

   B. -6 and -2

   C. 6 and 2

   D. $-6 \pm \dfrac{\sqrt{136}}{4}$

   E. Imaginary answer

11. Solve $|x - 7| = 1$

   A. $|x| = 8$

   B. $|x| = 6$

   C. $x = 8$

   D. $x = -6$

   E. $x = 6, 8$

12. $x = |7 - 26| = ?$

    A. -10

    B. 12

    C. 19

    D. -19

    E. None of the above

13. Which of the following is the correct graph of $-(x-1) > 3$

    A.

    B.

    C.

    D.

    E. None of the above

14. Find the simultaneous solution for $\begin{aligned} y &= 4x + 7 \\ y &= 2x + 4 \end{aligned}$

    A. $(-\frac{2}{3}, 1)$

    B. $(-\frac{3}{2}, 1)$

    C. $(-\frac{2}{3}, 2)$

    D. $(-2, 1)$

    E. $(\frac{2}{3}, 1)$

15. At what y coordinate do the following equations intersect?

$y = 3x$
$y = 6x - 2$

A. 6

B. 5

C. 4

D. 3

E. 2

16. At what x coordinate do the following equations intersect?

$y = x - 1$
$y = 2x + 1$

A. –2

B. –1

C. 0

D. 1

E. 2

17. Find the simultaneous solution for $\begin{aligned} y &= 3x \\ y &= 7x - 1 \end{aligned}$

A. $(\frac{3}{4}, \frac{1}{4})$

B. $(\frac{1}{4}, \frac{3}{4})$

C. $(4, 3)$

D. $(4, 1)$

E. $(3, 1)$

18. Which of the following is the correct graph of $\begin{array}{c} y \geq x \\ y \geq -x \end{array}$?

A.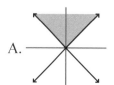

B.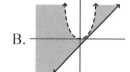

C.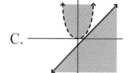

D.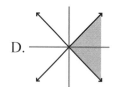

19. Which of the following is the correct graph of $\begin{array}{c} y > x^2 \\ y \leq x+1 \end{array}$?

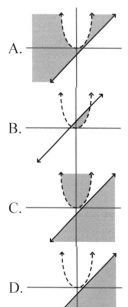

A.

B.

C.

D.

20. Solve for y if $y^x = 3$

    A. $y = 10^{\frac{x}{3}}$

    B. $y = 3^{\frac{x}{10}}$

    C. $y = 3^{\frac{10}{x}}$

    D. $y = 10^{\frac{\log 3}{x}}$

    E. $y = 10^{3x}$

21. Solve for y if $x^y = 10$

    A. $y = \dfrac{10}{\log x}$

    B. $y = \dfrac{\log x}{10}$

    C. $y = 10 \log x$

    D. $y = \log x$

    E. $y = \dfrac{1}{\log x}$

22. Which of the following is the correct graph of $\begin{array}{l} y > 3x \\ y < -3x \end{array}$

A.

B.

C.

D.

E. None of the above

23. Solve for y if $\log(y^x) = 1$

    A. $y = 10^{\frac{x}{10}}$

    B. $y = 10^{\frac{1}{x}}$

    C. $y = 10^x$

    D. $y = x^{10}$

    E. $y = 1^x$

24. Solve for y if $\log(y^x + 10) = 1$

    A. $y = 10^{\frac{x}{10}}$

    B. $y = 10^{\frac{1}{x}}$

    C. $y = 10^x$

    D. $y = x^{10}$

    E. $y = 1^x$

25. Which of the following correctly graphs $y > x^2 - 1$?

A.

B.

C.

D.

E. None of the above

SECTION 3: FUNCTIONS AND THEIR PROPERTIES

1. What is a function?

    A. A systematic manner in which to find a value.

    B. A specific type of graph, with exponents and logarithms.

    C. A specific type of graph, which cannot have exponents or logarithms.

    D. An equation which can have any characteristics.

    E. None of the above

2. What is the domain of a function?

    A. The x values that can be input into an equation.

    B. The x values that cannot be put into an equation.

    C. The type of graph that the function produces.

    D. The y values that cannot be put into an equation.

    E. The y values that can be input into an equation.

3. What is the Vertical Line Test used to determine?

    A. Whether or not the graph has a defined slope.

    B. If a graph is a vertical line.

    C. If a graph is a horizontal line.

    D. Whether or not a graph represents a function.

    E. There is no such thing as the Vertical Line Test.

4. What is the range of a function?

    A. The x values that can be input into an equation.

    B. The x values that cannot be put into an equation.

    C. The type of graph that the function produces.

    D. The y values that cannot be put into an equation.

    E. The y values that can be input into an equation.

5. Which of the following is NOT true?

   A. A function can have many output values for each value input.

   B. To find the square of a number you must multiply it by itself.

   C. Range is a measure of the y values an equation produces.

   D. Domain is a measure of the x values an equation allows.

   E. All of the above statements are true.

6. Which of the following graphs is linear?

   A.

   B.

   C.

   D.

7. Which of the following graphs is quadratic?

   A.

   B.

   C.

   D.

8. Which of the following graphs is exponential?

A.

B.

C.

D.

9. Which of the following functions is quadratic?

A. $y = 3^{x+1} - 5$

B. $y = \log(x+1) - 2$

C. $y = x^2 + 2$

D. $y = 14x - 7$

E. None of the above

10. Which of the following is exponential?

A. $y = 3^{x+1} - 5$

B. $y = \log(x+1) - 2$

C. $y = x^2 + 2$

D. $y = 14x - 7$

E. None of the above

11. Which of the following is linear?

A. $y = 3^{x+1} - 5$

B. $y = \log(x+1) - 2$

C. $y = x^2 + 2$

D. $y = 14x - 7$

E. None of the above

12. Which of the following is logarithmic?

    A. $y = 3^{x+1} - 5$

    B. $y = \log(x+1) - 2$

    C. $y = x^2 + 2$

    D. $y = 14x - 7$

    E. None of the above

13. Which of the following is not a function?

    A.

    B.

    C.

    D.

    E.

14. Which of the following is the graph of an absolute value?

    A.

    B.

    C.

    D.

    E.

For problems 15-16 consider the equation $y = \dfrac{1}{\sqrt{x+1}}$

15. What is the domain?

   A. $(0,3)$
   B. $(1,\infty)$
   C. $(-\infty,\infty)$
   D. $(-\infty,0)$
   E. $(1,°\ )$

16. What is the range?

   A. $(0,3)$
   B. $(1,\infty)$
   C. $(-\infty,\infty)$
   D. $(-\infty,0)$
   E. $(1,°\ )$

For problems 17-18 consider the equation $y = \dfrac{1}{x-1}$

17. What is the domain?

   A. $(1,\infty)$
   B. $(-\infty,1)\cup(1,\infty)$
   C. $(-\infty,-1)\cup(-1,\infty)$
   D. $(-\infty,\infty)$
   E. None of the above

18. What is the range?

   A. $(1,\infty)$
   B. $(-\infty,1)\cup(1,\infty)$
   C. $(-\infty,-1)\cup(-1,\infty)$
   D. $(-\infty,\infty)$
   E. None of the above

For problems 19-21 determine the y intercept of the equation.

19. $y = 3x - 4$

    A. –4

    B. 0

    C. 2

    D. 4

    E. 12

20. $y = 12 + 2x$

    A. –4

    B. 0

    C. 2

    D. 4

    E. 12

21. $y = x^2$

    A. –4

    B. 0

    C. 2

    D. 4

    E. 12

22. What is the inverse of $f(x) = x^2 + 1$?

    A. $\sqrt{x-1}$

    B. $x + 2$

    C. $\sqrt{x+1}$

    D. $x - 2$

    E. $\sqrt{x+2}$

23. What is the inverse of $f(x) = x^2 - 1$?

    A. $\sqrt{x-1}$

    B. $x+2$

    C. $\sqrt{x+1}$

    D. $x-2$

    E. $\sqrt{x+2}$

24. What is the inverse of $f(x) = x + 2$?

    A. $\sqrt{x-1}$

    B. $x+2$

    C. $\sqrt{x+1}$

    D. $x-2$

    E. $\sqrt{x+2}$

25. What is the inverse of $f(x) = x - 2$?

    A. $\sqrt{x-1}$

    B. $x+2$

    C. $\sqrt{x+1}$

    D. $x-2$

    E. $\sqrt{x+2}$

26. What is demonstrated by the graph below?

    A. A horizontal translation

    B. A vertical translation

    C. Symmetry about the y-axis

    D. Symmetry about the x-axis

    E. Symmetry about the origin

27. What is demonstrated by the graph below?

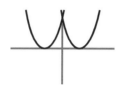

    A. A horizontal translation

    B. A vertical translation

    C. Symmetry about the y-axis

    D. Symmetry about the x-axis

    E. Symmetry about the origin

28. $f(x) = x^2$ is symmetric about the _____?

    A. x-axis

    B. origin

    C. line x=1

    D. line y=1

    E. y-axis

For problems 29-30 use $\begin{aligned} f(x) &= 5x + 7 \\ g(x) &= 3x - 2 \end{aligned}$

29. Determine $f(x) + g(x)$

    A. $8x + 9$

    B. $2x + 5$

    C. $2x + 9$

    D. $8x + 5$

    E. $\dfrac{5}{3}x - \dfrac{7}{2}$

30. Determine $f(x) - g(x)$

    A. $8x + 9$

    B. $2x + 5$

    C. $2x + 9$

    D. $8x + 5$

    E. $\dfrac{5}{3}x - \dfrac{7}{2}$

SECTION 4: NUMBER SYSTEMS AND OPERATIONS

For questions 1-4 use the following set of numbers:

$$\{1, 3, \neq, \sqrt{3}, 0, \frac{15}{4}\}$$

1. Identify all of the natural numbers in the set.

    A. 1, 3

    B. 0, 1, 3

    C. $0, 1, 3, \dfrac{15}{4}$

    D. $\neq, \sqrt{3}$

    E. None of the above

2. Identify all of the rational numbers in the set.

    A. 1, 3

    B. 0, 1, 3

    C. $0, 1, 3, \dfrac{15}{4}$

    D. $\neq, \sqrt{3}$

    E. None of the above

3. Identify all of the irrational numbers in the set.

   A. 1, 3

   B. 0, 1, 3

   C. $0, 1, 3, \dfrac{15}{4}$

   D. $\neq, \sqrt{3}$

   E. None of the above

4. Identify all of the complex numbers in the set.

   A. 1, 3

   B. 0, 1, 3

   C. $0, 1, 3, \dfrac{15}{4}$

   D. $\neq, \sqrt{3}$

   E. None of the above

5. Add $(3i + 4) + (4i - 2)$

   A. $7i + 2$

   B. $7i - 2$

   C. $7i + 6$

   D. $-7i + 6$

   E. $-i + 6$

6. Subtract $(3i + 6) - (6i - 4)$

   A. $3i + 10$

   B. $9i + 10$

   C. $-3i + 10$

   D. $-3i + 2$

   E. Operation cannot be performed

7. Multiply $i(2i+1)$

   A. $i-\sqrt{2}$

   B. $-i-2$

   C. $-i+2$

   D. $i+2$

   E. $i-2$

8. Simplify $\dfrac{(i+3)}{(i-3)}$

   A. $\dfrac{6i+4}{10}$

   B. $\dfrac{6i+4}{3i+9}$

   C. $\dfrac{6i+8}{3i+9}$

   D. $-\dfrac{6i+8}{10}$

   E. $\dfrac{9i+8}{10}$

9. Which of the following describes $1,2,3,4,5,6...$?

   A. Infinite set

   B. Geometric sequence

   C. Arithmetic sequence

   D. Finite set

   E. Infinite geometric series

10. Which of the following describes $1,2,4,8,16...$?

    A. Infinite set

    B. Geometric sequence

    C. Arithmetic sequence

    D. Finite set

    E. Infinite geometric series

11. What is a sequence?

   A. A function defined on the set of positive integers.

   B. A function defined on the set of negative integers.

   C. A function defined on the set of irrational numbers.

   D. A function defined on the set of natural numbers.

   E. A function defined on the set of whole numbers.

12. What is a series?

   A. The sum of the terms of a sequence.

   B. The difference of the terms of a sequence.

   C. The product of the terms of a sequence.

   D. The quotient of the terms of a sequence.

   E. The determinant of the terms of a sequence.

13. $4! = ?$

   A. 0

   B. 8

   C. 6

   D. 12

   E. 24

14. $0! = ?$

   A. 0

   B. 1

   C. 2

   D. 10

   E. Not possible

15. Simplify $6(5)!$ (keep in factorial form)

   A. 720

   B. $\dfrac{6}{5}!$

   C. $\dfrac{5}{6}!$

   D. $6!$

   E. $30!$

16. Expand $(v+r)^4$

   A. $v^4 + 4v^3r + 6v^2r + 4vr^3 + r^4$

   B. $v^4 + 4v^3r + 6v^2r^2 + 4vr^3 + r^4$

   C. $v^4 + 4vr + 6v^2r^2 + 4vr^3 + r^4$

   D. $v^4 + 4v^3r + 6v^2r^2 + r^4$

   E. $v^4 + 6v^2r^2 + 4vr^3 + r^4$

17. Expand $(x+y)^3$

   A. $x^3 + 3x^2y + 3xy^2 + y^3$

   B. $3x^2y + 3xy^2 + y^3$

   C. $x^3 + 3x^2y + 3xy + y^3$

   D. $x^3 + 3x^2y + 3xy^2 + xy + y^3$

   E. $x^3 + 3xy^2 + y^3$

18. Find the determinant of $\begin{bmatrix} 3 & 2 \\ 1 & 6 \end{bmatrix}$

   A. 0

   B. 12

   C. 16

   D. –21

   E. –9

19. Find the determinant of $\begin{bmatrix} 3 & 2 \\ 3 & -5 \end{bmatrix}$

    A. 0

    B. 12

    C. 16

    D. −21

    E. −9

20. Find the determinant of $\begin{bmatrix} 3 & -5 \\ 3 & 2 \end{bmatrix}$

    A. 0

    B. 12

    C. 16

    D. −21

    E. 21

🎓 Answer Key

Section 1: Algebraic Operations

1. B	8. D	15. B	22. A
2. D	9. C	16. B	23. D
3. A	10. B	17. A	24. C
4. C	11. E	18. C	25. B
5. E	12. A	19. B	
6. A	13. C	20. E	
7. A	14. D	21. A	

Section 2: Equations and Inequalities

1. E	8. D	15. E	22. C
2. D	9. A	16. A	23. B
3. A	10. E	17. B	24. E
4. C	11. E	18. A	25. B
5. B	12. C	19. B	
6. C	13. C	20. D	
7. C	14. B	21. E	

Section 3: Functions and Their Properties

1. A	9. C	17. B	25. B
2. A	10. A	18. D	26. E
3. D	11. D	19. A	27. A
4. E	12. B	20. E	28. E
5. A	13. E	21. B	29. D
6. C	14. C	22. A	30. C
7. B	15. E	23. C	
8. D	16. C	24. D	

Section 4: Number Systems and Operations

1. A	6. C	11. A	16. B
2. C	7. E	12. A	17. A
3. D	8. D	13. E	18. C
4. E	9. C	14. B	19. D
5. A	10. B	15. D	20. E

Test Taking Strategies

Here are some test-taking strategies that are specific to this test and to other CLEP tests in general:

- Keep your eyes on the time. Pay attention to how much time you have left.
- Read the entire question and read all the answers. Many questions are not as hard to answer as they may seem. Sometimes, a difficult sounding question really only is asking you how to read an accompanying chart. Chart and graph questions are on most CLEP tests and should be an easy free point.
- If you don't know the answer immediately, the new computer-based testing lets you mark questions and come back to them later if you have time.
- Read the wording carefully. Some words can give you hints to the right answer. There are no exceptions to an answer when there are words in the question such as always, all or none. If one of the answer choices includes most or some of the right answers, but not all, then that is not the answer. Here is an example:

> The primary colors include all of the following:
> A) Red, Yellow, Blue, Green
> B) Red, Green, Yellow
> C) Red, Orange, Yellow
> D) Red, Yellow, Blue
> E) None of the above

Although item A includes all the right answers, it also includes an incorrect answer, making it incorrect. If you didn't read it carefully, were in a hurry, or didn't know the material well, you might fall for this.

- Make a guess on a question that you do not know the answer to. There is no penalty for an incorrect answer. Eliminate the answer choices that you know are incorrect. For example, this will let your guess be a 1 in 3 chance instead.

What Your Score Means

Based on your score, you may, or may not, qualify for credit at your specific institution. At University of Phoenix, a score of 50 is passing for full credit. At Utah Valley State College, the score is unpublished, the school will accept credit on a case-by-case basis. Another school, Brigham Young University (BYU) does not accept CLEP credit. To find out what score you need for credit, you need to get that information from your school's website or academic advisor.

You can score between 20 and 80 on any CLEP test. Some exams include percentile ranks. Each correct answer is worth one point. You lose no points for unanswered or incorrect questions.

Test Preparation

How much you need to study depends on your knowledge of a subject area. If you are interested in literature, took it in school, or enjoy reading then your studying and preparation for the literature or humanities test will not need to be as intensive as someone who is new to literature.

This book is much different than the regular CLEP study guides. This book actually teaches you the information that you need to know to pass the test. If you are particularly interested in an area, or you want more information, do a quick search online. We've tried not to include too much depth in areas that are not as essential on the test. Everything in this book will be on the test. It is important to understand all major theories and concepts listed in the table of contents. It is also very important to know any bolded words.

Don't worry if you do not understand or know a lot about the area. With minimal study, you can complete and pass the test.

Legal Note

FLASHCARDS

This section contains flashcards for you to use to further your understanding of the material and test yourself on important concepts, names or dates. Read the term or question then flip the page over to check the answer on the back. Keep in mind that this information may not be covered in the text of the study guide. Take your time to study the flashcards, you will need to know and understand these concepts to pass the test.

Terms

Algebraic expression

Like or unlike terms?
2y, 14y

Like or unlike terms?
2y, -14x

Like or unlike terms?
14, -14

Like or unlike terms?
3x², 3x

Coefficient of the variable

Polynomial

Collection of terms that are separated by arithmetic operations

Numbers and variables

Unlike

Like

Unlike

Like

Expression containing the sum of a finite number of terms

The number multiplied by the variable

FOIL	Factor
Simplify	Algebraic equation
Balance in equations	Quadratic equation
What is the solution to a quadratic equation?	Vertex

Two numbers or terms that when multiplied together yield the original term

First, out, inner, last

Must contain an equal sign

Solve or reduce

$$\frac{-b \pm \sqrt{b^2 - 4ac}}{2a}$$

The value of each side of the equation is the same

The lowest point on the parabola

The root of the polynomial $ax^2+bx+c=0$

In graphing the term
x runs horizontal or
vertical?

In graphing the term
y runs horizontal or
vertical?

What is absolute value?

| |

≠

≥

≥

<

Vertical	Horizontal
Notation for absolute value	The distance between a number and 0 on the number line
Notation of less than or equal to	Notation for not equal to
Notation for less than	Notation for greater than or equal to

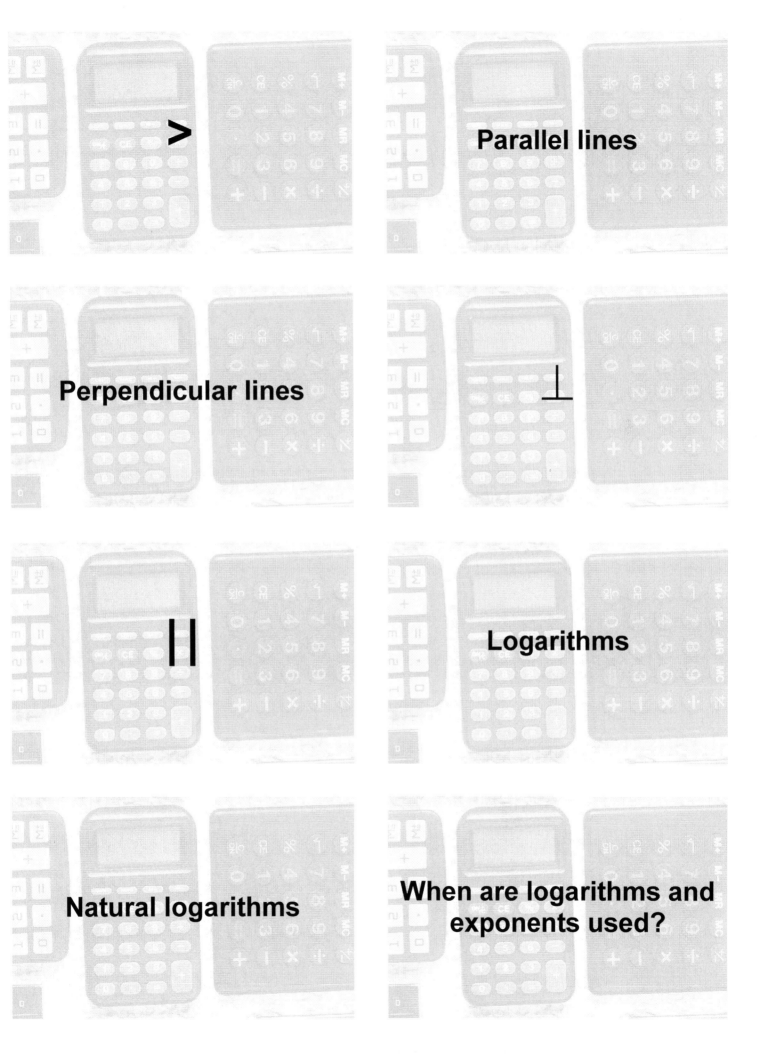

>

Parallel lines

Perpendicular lines

⊥

‖

Logarithms

Natural logarithms

When are logarithms and exponents used?

Two lines are parallel if they lie on the same plane and never intersect

Notation for greater than

Notation for perpendicular

Two lines are perpendicular if their intersection forms a right angle

The exponent of a positive number

Notation for parallel

To calculate simple & compound interest and exponential growth

Have a base "e" which is a constant

I = Prt

In I=Prt what does P stand for?

In I=Prt what does r stand for?

In I=Prt what does I stand for?

In I=Prt what does t stand for?

Set

{ }

Another name for empty set

Principle or principle amount	Simple interest
Interest earned	Annual interest rate
Collection of elements	Time
Null set	Empty set

Made in United States
Orlando, FL
09 January 2025

57055148R00061